LIVING WITH NATURE AT HAWK'S NEST

Enhancing The Seven Upland Habitats

By John Tomikel

Living close to nature is a spiritual experience. We are a part of the environment and not apart from it. The following work is a summary of experiences with animals and plants on twenty seven acres of land in Northwest Pennsylvania.- John Tomikel, Hawk's Nest, 2007

ISBN 978 1512360516 and 1512360511

Allegheny Press

The original text of this work appeared in 2007 without illustrations. The text has not been modified in order to keep its original integrity but a few photographs have been added to enhance its charm. A brief update appears at the end of the original text.

Bear dog in the field.

Topics

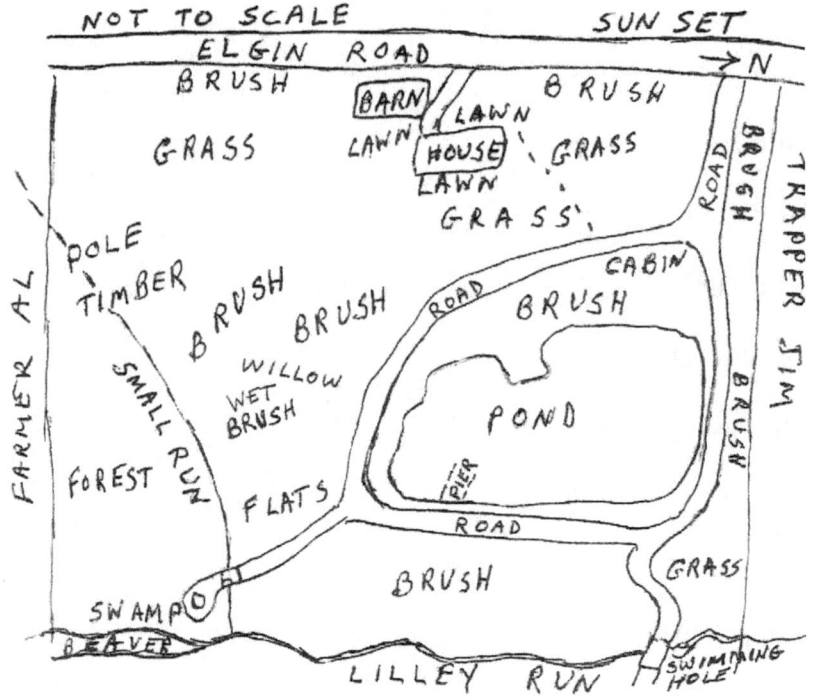

WESTERN HALF OF HAWK'S NEST

HAWK'S NEST

Hawk's Nest is the name I gave to our property. It has a double meaning. There was a Red-tailed Hawk nesting on the property when it was first purchased and Hawk was the name of my alter ego featured in many of my primitive man poems.

We are located about fifteen miles east of where the 80 degree West Longitude line crosses 42 degrees North Latitude. Our property is mostly in a valley created by a creek eroding through and reworking glacial deposits. The creek, Lilley Run, is four feet wide in most places during the dry periods of late summer. There is a highway bridge across the creek one-mile upstream and a highway bridge across the creek one mile downstream. Hawk's Nest is between the two bridges and accessible on narrow paved Elgin Road.

Elgin Road marks the west line of the property and the east line runs along an old railroad bed. The railroad was operating when the property was first purchased but after three years it ceased operation and the tracks, ties, and gravel bed were removed leaving behind a cinder road bed. A neighbor across the railroad bed eventually purchased the railroad section and blocked the entrances to deter motor bikers. The strategy didn't work too well since we often hear the sound of motor bikes as we take long walks in our deeper woods.

Our north line borders the property of Jim and his wife Marge. Their five children have since moved on to start their own families. On the other side of Jim's was Elmer and his wife who were in the dairy farming business when we first moved here but have since sold out to the Pennsylvania Game Commission and his property is now a State Gamelands.

On our south line the neighbors were Al and Grace who were also in the dairy business when we first moved here. Al passed away a few years ago and the property is occupied by Grace, who quit the dairy business. On the other side of Farmer Al's is Jerry and his wife Barbara who had five school age children when we moved here but their children have also gone to their adult marriages and pursuits.

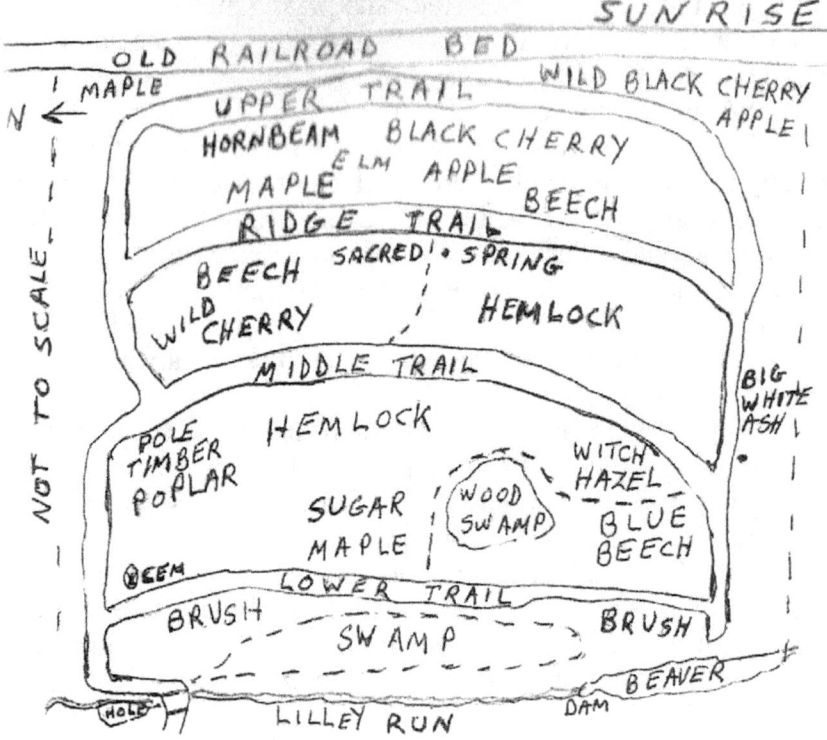

EASTERN HALF OF HAWK'S NEST

So there are now four families living in the valley which was once used for dairy farming. The remnants of farming are abundant grassland, which is going into brush before our very eyes. Except for the Game Commission we are all keeping large parcels of our land in grass by mowing some sections at least once in every two years.

January: The barn, house, and cabin taken from the big pond. April stands on the ice which was nine inches thick on this day.

Hawk's Nest comprises 27 acres of land. The entire valley between the two bridges encompasses about 348 acres bounded by the paved road, two bridges and an old railroad bed. The outside of this perimeter consists mostly of big woods. As we approach the nearby towns there are scattered houses and some farmland, which supplies us with fresh vegetables in the growing season and we are especially fond of the sweet corn and tomatoes grown there.

Bonnie and I were living in Washington County south of Pittsburgh. Pennsylvania when we decided to purchase property that would give us access to Lake Erie and its recreational benefits. I consulted a realtor who was taking me to a property near Union City. It was semi-developed property located on the South Branch of French Creek. As we passed Hawk's Nest he said it was property listed with him and it was mostly swamp, a property I would not like.

This was exactly what I wanted. A month later we owned 25 acres of wetland. The next summer I built a cabin on the property. Later we purchased two more acres from Farmer Al and constructed our house on it. However for five years before that we visited the cabin and then lived in it the year we built the house.

When we moved to Hawk's Nest our family consisted of me, wife Bonnie, her parents Irene and Everett, and daughter April who was one year old when we moved into the cabin. We also had our small dog Lobo. Five years later we were blessed with our son Matthew. After Lobo perished we acquired our larger dog Bear.

Our dog Lobo weighed twenty pounds, was black and white and had a spaniel tail. We originally found her as a puppy trapped in a dewberry patch on the side of the road. She was probably the runt of the litter and someone had abandoned her.

She became Everett's dog and they roamed the woods together. When Everett fished in the creek, Lobo was there to leap up at each catch.

Lobo developed a heart condition and the veterinarian prescribed medicine to alleviate the problem. Everett nursed her faithfully and she still followed him on his daily walks. Sometimes she would faint and he would carry her back to her bed in the basement of the house.

One morning Everett found Lobo dead. She had pulled Everett's jacket from the chair where he kept it and had curled on it.

Everett picked out a spot in the open woods on the banks of our little creek that flowed into Lilley Run. We buried Lobo there and I carved LOBO on a flat stone to put over her resting place. Two years later it was Everett's turn to die. He was cremated and his ashes were entombed in a cement slab next to Lobo. A World War II veteran's memorial plaque marks the spot.

A few years after that on a cold February morning when the temperature was minus fourteen degrees Fahrenheit a small male puppy showed up on our basement patio. I assumed it was a stray or perhaps dropped off. We didn't want another dog at that time. However, I did put some bread out for it and watched it huddled on the cement shivering. The next day it followed Matthew to the school bus. It stayed on the basement patio and when the bus arrived after school it gleefully ran up to greet Matt.

Against my better judgment I kept feeding the dog and he kept shivering out on the patio. I was tempted to call the county dog officer but we were getting fond of the animal.

After two weeks a man came to the house in a pick-up truck and said, "I understand you have my dog." He opened the door on the passenger side and the dog jumped in. Matt had already named him "gray wolf."

I told the man I would buy the dog from him and he said the dog was not for sale because his children wanted to keep it. He said it was part "blue tick" or Australian sheep dog. We were all somewhat downhearted.

About a week after that episode the man returned with the dog and said we could have it. The dog's name was Bear. I offered him money but he refused to take it.

I made a bed for Bear in the barn and locked him up every night. When Matt went to the school bus he let Bear out. Bear was there to greet him when he returned from school. Later I fenced in a large section around the barn and cut an entrance door into the side of the barn for Bear. He now had a large area to roam, as well as a warm bed, before he was released each morning.

Hawk's Nest has a lot of wild animals and plants, but it is not wilderness, which is an environment with only a small touch of humanity. We have to accept the fact that economic, political and recreational demands are slowly, but surely, shrinking the world's limited wilderness areas. There was hope at one time that national forest legislation would help preserve much of these areas in the United States, but that is not the situation.

Most conservationists have the philosophy of "wise use" and "sustained yields" which seems to be a pragmatic approach considering our population is increasing at alarming rates and demanding greater access to these wild areas. Foot travel in wild areas is giving way to mechanization, which limits the spiritual value of wild places. It is difficult to contemplate and relate to the Creation while riding on a motor bike and having the sound of a motor droning in the air.

Hawk's Nest is a remnant of the wilderness that once was. Its flora and fauna are a learning laboratory and one can easily communicate with nature in its isolated surroundings. Plants and animals seem to arrive out of nowhere. They take hold in one section and migrate slowly to some other section of the property where they may thrive in large numbers.

The animal and plant populations fluctuate noticeably over a year period. One species may disappear for several years and suddenly appear again as if by magic. Perhaps they go into hiding, but remain on the property or go to adjoining properties. At this time our disappearing species include the smooth green snake, box turtle, black billed cuckoo, nighthawk, and red fox. It has been a while since I have seen them.

We were still living in the cabin when Everett told me to accompany him to the bridge. When we arrived he pointed to a three foot long green snake entwined in a small blue beech tree that was growing along the creek. It stayed in that location for about a week before it disappeared. It was probably a rough green snake since they are climbers while the smooth green snake stays pretty much on the ground.

We didn't see another green snake until two years later when a small one appeared in the driveway under a vehicle. I picked it up and put it in the newly created butterfly garden. A couple of days later a small slightly brown green snake appeared at the cement pad leading into the barn. When it saw me it went into a hole between the pad and the barn. I noticed at least two different snakes there throughout most of the summer. Now they seem to be gone from that area. That was twenty years ago and we haven't seen any at the barn since.

After we moved permanently to Hawk's Nest we were treated at least once every summer to a flock of nighthawks doing their swirls and acrobatic dives through the air. When Farmer Al got rid of his cattle there were no annual summer nighthawk visits. There was also a decrease in the local fly population and the two are probably related. The nighthawk *(Chordeiles minor)* is not a hawk but a species of goatsucker.

There have been other transient species that have passed through in some years and not in others. In this category are the bobcat and whistling swan. The secretive bobcat might still be around. There was also a pure white dove that roosted on the deck railing for three days. It looked like the doves that magicians use in their acts. Other species in this category will be mentioned in other sections of this work.

So we live from day to day with many different plants and animals housed in what could be classified as wild land. Like the conservationists and wildlife managers whom I often criticize I try to maintain different environments and this takes a constant manipulation of nature. If I didn't do this, the land would revert to forest and the creatures that live in our swamp, grassland, brush, and pond would have to move on or perish.

One cannot take an animal such as a chipmunk and study it in isolation. The chipmunk is connected to other animals as predator and as prey. It uses a variety of plants and other animals in its life style. When we study the chipmunk and the animals related to it, and the animals related to those animals, we have an appreciation for the "web of life." This is the situation we perceive at Hawk's Nest.

The same situation exists with plants. There is a process by which pioneer plants prepare and condition the soil for other plants that will follow. The sun-loving plants grow to provide an environment for the shade tolerant plants, which eventually mature and crowd out the sun tolerant plants.

At Hawk's Nest it may not be feasible to make assumptions about other places on earth. I cannot equate what happens in the Amazon rainforest, the western prairie, or even the Southern Pine regions with observations at Hawk's Nest. Of course, I have traveled to or read about other places and I could understand the succession of plants or the relationships of predators and prey in those far places and relate those to Hawk's Nest and come up with some theory on the laws of nature. For now, I am content to observe what I have before me and record what I observe.

The Magnificent Seven

We were fortunate in the acquisition of Hawk's Nest since it contained the seven different environments peculiar to land which are grassland, brush, pole timber, and forest of soil habitats and swamp, pond, and creek of water habitats. This provided me with enough material, a sort of natural history of Hawk's Nest, to write an outdoor column, *"The Outdoorsman,"* which appeared in the *Erie Morning News* as well as nature features for the *Erie Sunday Times.* The columns ran for fourteen years with as many as three columns in some weeks due to an offshoot called *-Letters to the Outdoorsman. "*

We had been living at Hawk's Nest for six years when I received a call from a former student who became a professor at the local Edinboro University. He informed me that there was a temporary opening in the Geosciences Department and asked if I would come out of retirement to teach the Conservation of Natural Resources for one year. I came out of retirement and the temporary position lasted for fourteen years. I finally retired at age seventy-five.

The Woodland Trails

There are about two miles of trails including mower roads on the property. Two main trails parallel the north and south property lines and these are connected to five crossover trails. These trails are also mower roads around the swamp and around our pond. Mowing these roads keeps us from getting too wet after a heavy rain as we take our daily walks.

The deep woods start at the edge of the floodplain of the creek and occupy the hillside up to the railroad bed. There are three walking trails in the deep woods. The lowest of these in elevation is the Middle Trail. It begins in the north among the poplars then winds around through hemlocks and comes out the south where it joins an elevated wet land. For now I will say the trails begin in the north and trend south. At the southern end of the Middle Trail is our giant white ash tree with a circumference of eleven feet and eight inches. Its height is one hundred and ten feet.

Further up the slope is the Ridge Trail that follows the crest of a glacial kame terrace. Water seeps are abundant just below this trail. This is where I cleared out a section of seep, filled it with gravel, banked it with clay, inserted a ten foot two inch pipe and created our "sacred spring."

Beech trees, many of them twenty or more inches in diameter, surround the Ridge Trail. Sometime in the past, several beech saplings fused together and created trees with diameters of three to four feet.

The Upper Trail parallels the old railroad bed and has the oldest trees on the property. In a forest such as this it would be rare that a tree reaches the age of two hundred years. Heavy snows, high winds, and shallow roots limit the age of the trees.

However, on the Upper Trail there are black cherry trees with diameters of thirty inches. We are told that these trees with a thirty-foot straight trunk may be worth four thousand dollars each. We have no intention of selling them.

There is an old butternut tree *(Juglans cinerea)* just off this trail. It is about eighty feet tall. On the other end of the Upper Trail are two bitternut hickory about the same height.

Between the butternut and the hickory there is a mix of beech, hornbeam, black cherry, maple and elm. The elms reach heights of sixty feet before they succumb to the disease peculiar to them. I cut these for firewood. One trunk was twenty inches in diameter and I carved a pagan statue out of it. The statue now stands at the entrance to the pier on the pond.

Interspersed among the trees of the Upper Trail are many old apple trees that have seen better days. These are about fifteen inches in diameter and forty feet high. Occasionally they produce fruit but mostly they use their energy to cling to life. Many of the side branch limbs are dead on the live trees and there are many dead apple trees that cast a haunting image as they occupy space among the living. Most of these apple trees are crusted with lichens and have moss growing on their bases.

After a heavy windstorm, of which there are many, it is common to find trees blown over with their roots spread like a peacock fan in the air. These are mostly shallow rooted hemlocks in the low wet areas. Often accompanying the blown hemlocks are poplars, which have grown too close to the hemlocks and are simply dragged down with them.

In the Middle and Ridge Trail areas the wind-damage is most likely only a loss of limbs. One large sugar maple was broken off about eight feet from the ground. Its trunk was twenty-nine inches in diameter and its age by ring count was ninety-two years. A large beech in this area had lost eight large limbs. It was caught in an early heavy wet snowfall before it shed its leaves. My neighbor Jerry said he would take the limbs since he was heating his house with wood at that time. A year had passed and he never took them so I cut them up for my own use.

GRASSLAND

We have about an acre in lawn where the grass is kept to four inches high. The lawn surrounds the house and the driveway. A mowed lawn is almost of no value to wildlife. It is basically a green desert although insects, the little brown snake, voles, and frogs may be found there. In summer, the fairy ring of mushrooms, puffballs, and the shaggy mane mushrooms will pop up from time to time. We often eat the puffballs and shaggy manes. The shaggy manes that we don't eat turn into inky ooze almost overnight.

Tree swallows, barn swallows, bluebirds and flycatchers scoop up insects as they fly above the lawn. Bats appear at night and work the area. For several weeks in mid-summer the lightning bugs light up the night. In late May and throughout June the June bugs rise up from the lawn and hit the screens on our windows. So the mowed area is not completely devoid of life or activity.

The lightning bug or firefly is an interesting study. The male flies through the air sending out its luminescent signal while the female rests in the grass. After mating the female will send out a false signal to fireflies of a different species and when they arrive, she eats them. Lightning bugs, or fireflies, are neither bugs nor flies, they are beetles.

Robins, flickers, starlings, cowbirds, grackles, and crows may be seen on any morning pecking in the short grass. Barn swallows will follow the mower as it kicks up insects lodging there. Moths emerge from the grass at night. We see them dancing in the beams of light emitted through the windows. And we see bats picking them off.

The real grassland at Hawk's Nest is in those areas that remain without mowing for some period of time, usually one growing season with an autumn mowing. This is mowing after the wildlife young have matured enough to get out of the way of the mower and return when mowing has been completed. The mowing is necessary if this land is to remain in grasses and low plants. The mower blade is set from five to six inches above the ground at this time.

There is one large field, which we named the whiffle ball field since we played that game there when the children were little. It is about an acre in size. There are three other large patches of grass, which are located around the swamp and along part of the creek. These swamp and creek patches are mostly grasses along with buttercup, forget-me-not, sneeze weed, skunk cabbage, dogbane, poison hemlock and colts foot. On the fringes of this grass are the tall goldenrod, Joe Pye Weed, ironweed, boneset, and blue vervain. These seem to be sentinels on guard protecting the lower plants inside their perimeter.

There is another area about a half-acre in size that borders Al's property. There are three bluebird boxes set up here. At least one bluebird nests here every season. At this time there is a tree swallow in one box and a yellow jacket nest in the other. The latter box is one made last winter and now that I look at it I see that I did not make the opening large enough for anything but a wren. The opening is three quarter inch when it should be at least a full inch. I will correct that at the end of the summer. Mice will probably live in all three boxes over the winter and I will evict them before the migrants arrive in spring.

As I write this I am thinking about the main field that I haven't mowed for three years. It now has brush trees five to seven feet tall consisting mostly of apple, red maple, hawthorn, wild black cherry, and sumac. Maintaining this area as a field is important and the shrubbery will have to be brush-hogged if the grassland is to be preserved.

The poplar is considered a nuisance tree in some areas. It spreads by sending out long roots just below the surface of the ground. When conditions are just right the roots will send up a shoot which will become a tree. The poplar is usually an interconnected system of roots and shoots that extend for many miles. One biologist claimed taiga is just one big poplar tree. The trees, other than poplar, can be contained by mowing or clearing with an ax.

This field area is home to rabbits that often hide there. Rabbits are often seen in the mowed areas. One rule of habitat maintenance is if you want more rabbits you have to do with fewer squirrels.

A casual walk through this main field reveals a profusion of flowering plants as well as forbs which are low growing succulents. Here can be found dandelions, Indian paint brush, cinquefoil, blue-eyed grass, Queen Anne's Lace,strawberry, mallow, basil, birds foot trefoil, yarrow, ironweed, red clover, white clover, and several different types of grasses.

In the cooler shadier and moister area are square stemmed monkey flower, peppermint, and nightshade. These seem to need more shelter than open field plants. Where there is shade, there is also more moisture. Where the grass meets the brush one finds the purple asters, goldenrod and pokeweed.

Besides the eastern cottontail rabbit these grassy areas are home to the meadow vole, jumping mouse, weasel and woodchuck. I have never seen the least weasel in the wild but every autumn some mysterious creature leaves several of them as well as dead shrews on the road leading to our mailbox. I have photographed many of these gifts laid along a six inch ruler for size. If it were not for the mysterious donor I would not be aware that these animals were around.

It causes me to wonder. How many animals were there in my surroundings that I was unaware of their existence. I know the fox was there because of tracks in the winter snow. The timberdoodle leaves its telltale holes in the wet mud. The owl leaves a regurgitated pellet. The skunk leaves its calling card and the black bear leaves its scat. What mysterious creatures exist around me that do not leave any evidence of their existence behind?

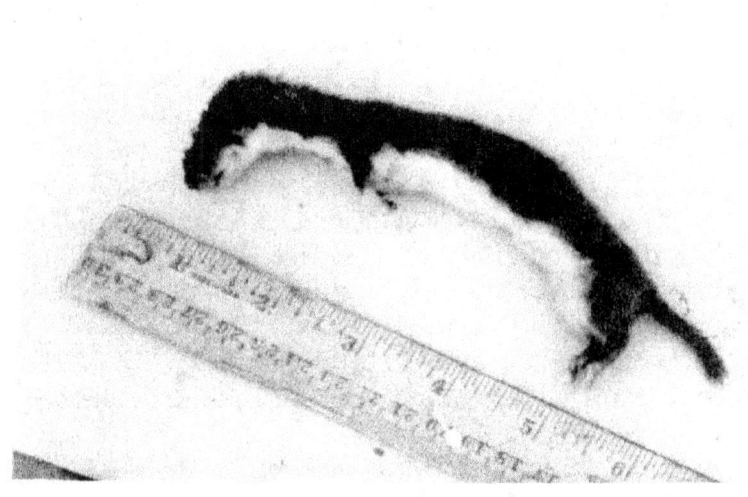

The least weasel is often deposited on the road by some unknown assailant.

The little brown snake inhabits the grass. It grows to thirteen inches and is easily seen by putting a board about a foot square on the grass. Return in two days and there will be a little brown snake under it. When we used the whiffle ball field we had to remove the snakes from under the bases before we began play.

The Brown Snake *(Storaria dekayi)* is easily captured and handled. It feeds mostly at night. Its food consists of earthworms, snails, slugs, insects, spiders and the small tree frog. Although it may live in moist areas I have found it mostly in the dry field. When I introduce youngsters to snakes at Hawk's Nest I usually let them handle the brown snake. When we used to let the house cats roam they would often bring home a little brown snake. When we opened the door they would rush into the house and release the snake, which gave us some problems. We didn't capture one brown snake for three days. It had taken up lodging under the kitchen cabinet baseboards.

Once the pond was constructed I ordered a load of bank gravel to give the road around it a firmer foundation. I would wheelbarrow the gravel to low spots and fill them in. Generally the sticking snow starts falling near the end of November and that is when my outdoor work is curtailed. One November I still had half of the ten-ton load of bank gravel in an accessible pile. I left it for the following spring.

When the snow melted in March I went to resume my wheeling and filling. I had my first load almost ready to go when I unearthed a sleeping jumping mouse and threw it on the load along with some of its nest. It was fast asleep. I gingerly picked it up and placed it back in the hole along with some extra leaves and grass then covered it with ten inches of loose fine gravel and soil. I checked the spot about once a week until the middle of April when it was obvious the jumper was afoot.

I am writing this in early June. Two days ago I kicked up a jumping mouse as I walked through the edge of the field. I assume they are well and thriving.

The Meadow Jumping Mouse (*Zapus hudsonius)* is the only hibernating mouse. Its total length is about nine inches with a five inch tail. It is also known as the Kangaroo Mouse since it has strong hind legs and is true to its name. However, it has no relationship to kangaroos.

The jumper does not make tunnels as do voles and other mice but relies on its leaps and speed to escape predators. It is found in the wet areas of our grasslands as well as in the newly growing small brush. I once observed one swimming in our frog pond. That is a dangerous area for a mouse since our large water snake hangs out there.

The meadow jumper is a seed eater. It also eats berries, new plant stems, and occasionally insects. A friend had seen one eating the coffee-like seeds of the curly dock.

We are very fortunate to have this beautiful little creature in our midst for they are not common. Like some other creatures one may go a lifetime without seeing one.

One very small jumping mouse leaped toward me as I was moving some brush to a brush pile. It was obviously running from something. It landed in a strand of dewberry vines and seemed to be stuck there. I was tempted to free it but did want to add to its stress. It wrestled with its entanglement for about four minutes before it finally broke free and bounced crazily into foot high hawthorn seedlings .

Rabbits

All animals, whether they walk, crawl, run, fly, or swim have basic specific needs. These are water, food, protection from enemies, and a place to raise their young. The trick to habitat management is to understand how a particular animal achieves these things. Once this is understood then the maximum habitat for a particular animal can be obtained.

Generally, we don't set out to create a habitat for a specific species. Some habitat is already there and we work on that environment, improving it for a species we fancy.

We have two distinct species of rabbits at Hawk's Nest, the Eastern Cottontail and the New England Cottontail. Generally, the Eastern Cottontail is a stronger species and it is pushing the New England Cottontail out of existence. We are at the western edge of the New England Cottontail range.

The New England Cottontail *(Sylvilagus transitionalis)* was first identified as a separate species in 1980. Since then, the Eastern Cottontail *(Sylvilagus floridanus)* has been moving into the New England's range.

The Eastern Cottontail can do with less food and is more durable than its competitor. However, neither rabbit has a long life span. The average rabbit only lives about nine months. A wild rabbit may live five years in captivity. When hunting groups transfer rabbits to their grounds they usually are disappointed since they most often don't survive to reproduce.

Differences in the rabbits are subtle. A New England is a darker brown and often has a black spot between its ears. It is smaller than the Eastern, which appears grayish and has a white streak.

Short of skeletal and skull measurements, rabbit droppings are the best indicators of which rabbit is in the area. The New England has around sixty pellets in its droppings and the Eastern less than twenty. Generally, the Eastern feeds at dawn or dusk while the New England only feeds at night. According to the location of the droppings at Hawk's Nest the New England seems to be in high brush on the edge of the forest and the Eastern in the low brush nearer to the grassland feeding ground.

The rabbits usually eat their first soft droppings since these are only partially digested. What we find are most often the second pass the droppings have made through the digestive system.

This young woodchuck started clicking his teeth at me when I approached.

Woodchuck aka Groundhog

We had an abundance of woodchucks *(Marmota monaz)* when we first began living at Hawk's Nest. They had entrances and exit holes at several locations in the high grass areas. Most of the grass area holes were connected to tunnels that led to adjoining brush areas.

Farmer Al was raising cattle next door and he did not appreciate the woodchuck burrows that dotted his main grazing areas and so did not object to chuck shooters eradicating them on his property. He was careful to instruct them in the location of the property boundaries. Our woodchuck population often spilled over onto his and he would mention it now and then. Perhaps he thought we should have encouraged the shooters.

Once while walking around the pond I came upon two woodchucks eating the white clover, which grows luxuriously on the mowed roads of the pond. One jumped into the pond and swam in a small circle then returned to land and disappeared into the brush. The other seemed to look at me with contempt. I tried to walk around him. I really didn't know its sex but will call it him for convenience. I moved to get around the guy and continue my walk. When I moved toward him the little bugger charged me with gnashing teeth that made a clacking chatter. I backed off. The little guy eyed me suspiciously. I tried walking around him a few more times and each time he came at me with his jaws clicking. It was more than scary but I didn't want to challenge the critter so I reversed my direction.

When I saw a live woodchuck in the grass in those early days I would often give a loud whistle and the chuck would stand up like a prairie dog and slowly turn its head. I tried to imitate the alarm whistle a chuck makes before it dives into its escape hole. For making this sound he has also earned the name of "whistle pig."

Ron Boone, a friend of mine, related a story about sitting on his porch and hearing a faint purring sound. After several days of catching the sound he was able to trace it to a chuck living under his porch. Ron lives in the city limits on a residential street that has large backyards.

A mature woodchuck is almost twenty inches long with a six-inch tail. It weighs about ten pounds but some individuals can reach fifteen pounds before hibernating. Its fur is soft to the touch but has no commercial value since it deteriorates rapidly. A description of the chuck physique would emphasize its heavy body, small ears, and short legs. Its tail is short when compared to other rodents.

Our woodchucks are most active in early morning and late afternoon. They hibernate in winter after some last minute gorging and fattening. Their extensive burrows and tunnels have several chambers with special uses of sleeping, raising the young, and defecation.

When two former college students of mine visited me one summer we walked around the property. I pointed out a large squirrel on a black cherry tree on the edge of one field. One of the students said it was a woodchuck. When we got closer I could see that he was correct. It was on a limb about twelve feet off the ground. I knew they could swim but didn't know they could climb trees.

These students were naturalists and employed with the state. One of them was into survival training. He and his father often spent cold winter days sleeping in their sleeping bags under a blanket of snow. I was quite impressed by this and some of his other stories. Often in the teaching game, I have learned as much from students as they have from me.

Woodchucks eat grass and this makes their flesh acceptable as food for meat eating animals. I have eaten them many times at wild food gatherings. Woodchuck and opossum usually no longer show up on the menu at these meetings since many participants no longer consider them as wild food. Most wild food meetings I attend are in West Virginia. Need I say more.

Woodchucks are a benefit to other animals. Their burrows are used by rabbits, skunks, and opossums, as well as the smaller mouse-sized creatures. Their burrows and tunnels drain off water during heavy rains and keep it in storage for soil

Unfortunately Bear dog is death to groundhogs. He has cleared them from the vicinity of the house and barn. He eats small ones immediately and clumsily tries to bury the larger ones. After a few days of stinking and attracting hordes of flies I usually take the dead chuck and bury it in a deep hole. I have to bury it deeply or else Bear dog will dig it up and I will find it around the front deck the next day. Bear will eat the entire chuck except for its stomach filled with greenery.

There is no shortage of woodchucks at Hawk's Nest or adjoining properties. At this writing a chuck has an entrance hole near the side of our number two field. The hole is easily located since it has a ring of clay and stones around it. These were tossed out of the burrow. The tunnel leads to a clump of sumac about fifteen feet away. In this thicket there are more holes but only one of them has the familiar ring of clay, stones, and earth around it. The other tunnel entrances are difficult to detect since they are devoid of the tell-tale earth rings. .

When we leave our driveway and proceed north on Elgin Road we see many animals darting in front of the car, Woodchucks are abundant along the road. We drive slowly and with caution until we reach the big bridge where there is a considerable decrease in the number of critters. The large number of road-kills suggest that some drivers must be hitting the animals deliberately.

I am writing this at ten-thirty p.m. and sitting propped up in my bed. It is a warm July evening and there is another creature lurking about. It is a skunk and its perfume is wafting through the screened open windows. It is out working on the lawn. It is a welcome visitor.

Skunk

There is no doubt when a skunk is visiting in the evening since we can identify the odor it brings with it. The next day we can find small funnel shaped holes in the lawn area. These are signs that the skunk has been digging for grubs.

Another sign that a skunk has been lurking about is a bee's nest destroyed in the ground. They eat the nest, bees, larva and combs but often leave enough of the nest to identify what happened there. A ground nest of yellow jackets constantly pestered me as I added cuttings to my large brush pile. I had to detour slightly around the area every time I dragged cut limbs to the pile. One day I found the nest dug up. The hole that the nest occupied was about four inches deep, four inches wide and ten inches long.

Bear dog had a faint skunk odor about him for a few days last spring. It was not strong but it was there. We lock him up at sundown and let him out when we go up to the road for the morning newspaper so he is not out when skunks are most active. However, he did bring a dead skunk home once. It was considerably deteriorated and had no strong odor about it. He probably rolled on the carcass which is what dogs like to do.

Skunks are at home in the city as well as in rural areas. Unfortunately they cannot elude an oncoming automobile. Many people consider skunks a natural enemy and may go out of their way to destroy them.

I have had many encounters with skunks in my life and I have never witnessed the skunk shooting out its defensive stream of liquid with its great sphincter muscles. One of the incidents of skunks in my life occurred when I had a summer job with a construction company that built suburban houses. There was a skunk in the basement of one of the houses when we showed up for work one day. Two of the older workers went into a frenzy looking for stones and rocks to hurl at the skunk. They eventually killed it. There was no reasoning with them even though I told them that skunks catch and eat rats, mice and chipmunks that were all evident in the building area. For the record, skunks also eat fruit, berries, birds, bird eggs, earthworms, grasshoppers, beetles, and crickets.

Our striped skunk (*Mephitis mephitis)* is a foot and a half long. Its bushy tail adds ten inches to its length. It has narrow white stripes on its black body. Mature skunks weigh about five pounds.

The skunk itself is the prey of great horned owls, foxes, bobcats, coyotes, and dogs. However, they are fearless and with a quick squirt will drive most enemies away.

Skunks will live almost anywhere, under a porch or in a burrow, usually a burrow excavated by other animals. One family occupied one of my bigger brush piles one winter. The pile foundation consisted of several six foot tree logs about ten inches in diameter. These were laid about two feet apart and a layer of sturdy limbs was put over them before smaller brush was piled on.

Two days ago there was a strong skunk odor in the air at night. The next day I found that another yellow jacket nest was dug up. This is the same yellow jacket nest I painfully avoided when I walked almost over it on my way to the pond.

There are few more pleasant sights than to see a mother skunk leading four or five little ones through an open field. This was the sight before our eyes one August evening when we got a whiff of skunk and went racing out in the night with our flashlights.

Meadow Vole

It is necessary to cut the two big fields at least once every two years if I am to maintain a grassland habitat. It seems better to cut the fields sometime in late August. This takes into consideration that the young animals have matured and the new tree seedlings have not become firmly established. The idea is not to change the grassland, but to maintain it as a viable habitat, an ecosystem.

The denizen of the grassland is the vole. Most people will simply refer to them as a "field mouse" and let it go at that. Moles differ from mice in that they have tiny black eyes and short ears that are almost hidden in its fur.

Voles can be seen running everywhere once the mowing begins. In all of the twenty-five years of mowing the big field at Hawk's Nest, I have never killed a vole. The blade is set high enough that it would pass over them unless they stand on their hind legs.

The meadow vole *(Microtus pennsylvanicus)* has a great role to fill in nature. It is at the bottom of the food chain and if it were not so prolific it probably would have been extinct long ago. One captive mole produced seventeen litters in one year. In the wild, voles reproduce once a month from May to November. Every meat eater including the least weasel, which is smaller than the average vole, eats voles.

At least once or twice a summer we see a Red-tailed hawk swoop down and land in the big field, pick up a vole or a brown snake and head back to the sky. Often the hawk pauses long enough for us to get a good look at it. One hawk ate the vole before it took off. Other hawks that we have seen come down in the big field are the Red-shouldered and Northern Harrier. We have also had one observation of a Broad-winged Hawk on an April day and a Sharp-shinned in October.

One of my reference books for children states that the hawk has sharp talons and a beak that are designed for ripping apart mice and other small creatures. The book gives the impression that this design was made with purposeful insight by some creator. The story should read that the hawks with sharp talons and beaks were more successful at gathering and eating food than those early hawks that did not have these advantages. The hawks with sharp talons and beaks were better adapted to survival.

It may not be far-fetched to say that the balance of nature depends on the shaggy brown meadow vole, which is only six inches long. Its tail is less than two inches long. If our vole crop failed there would be repercussions throughout our valley. Those predators that depend on voles would shift to other species such as chickens. If the voles are gone then the predators must find other food sources or starve.

Go to any of our grasslands and spread the grass apart and you will find the pathways of the vole. These are roads that lead to food and safety. Some of the paths lead to tunnels and nests.

The vole nest is a round hollow ball about the size of a softball. It is wedged in a clump of grass tightly woven. The voles own body heat will get it through the coldest winter as it lives and moves under the snow. Many of the nests are partly buried in the earth.

When the winter snow melts and the grass has been flattened by the weight of the snow the vole runways become evident. They criss-cross in the field is like a major highway Voles live comfortably under the snow foraging for hay like so many miniature cattle. When the hay is not at hand the vole will gnaw on the bark of tree seedlings. Thus, it is important for me to place plastic guards at the base of young fruit trees. The plastic guard also has to be tall enough to discourage rabbits.

A winter without much snow is a disaster to the resident vole population. They are exposed to the winter predators. Feral cats and dogs come to the big field in winter and work the areas without snow. Once we obtained our dog Bear, the cats quit coming around.

Hairy-tailed Mole

There is a small moist area near the creek that I keep mowed at three inches. It is almost forty by forty feet square and slopes down toward the creek. At one time it was covered with dense black willow, but I dug the willow out down to ground level where I could not get at the roots for many different reasons. Mowing has kept the willows at bay. This spot is a clearing as we approach the creek. We can see ducks on the creek shore before they see us. This spot is also home to moles.

The hairy-tailed mole *(Parascalops breweri)* makes tunnels through the wet earth and creates abundant molehills. Both of our dogs have dug into the hills with gusto. They were not successful in catching a mole except for one incident when Lobo cocked her ears and listened, scratched, dug, then came up with a mole. Bear dog has gotten moles in other areas. He does not eat them.

A mole on the surface of the ground is helpless. It is out of its ecological protective niche. It lives in the root zone of grasses where it constantly tunnels in search of food. The white grubs of June bugs are like dessert to the mole whose main food is earthworms. They will also eat snails, spiders, beetles and other insects.

There is no day and night to the mole. It is active at all hours with its large front digging claws propelling it through the earth. Mice and shrews often use the tunnels that the mole leaves behind.

The hairy-tailed mole is six inches long and has short legs. A lucky mole will live to be four years old in the wild. Most small animals in the wild have, at most, a two-year life span regulated by predators, disease, and incidents related to weather.

BRUSH AND BRAMBLES

The brush area of Hawk's Nest takes up two to three acres depending on measurement and classification. It consists of woody plants three to ten feet tall. The biggest brush area can be seen from the kitchen and dining room windows. It begins at the edge of the mowed house area and extends down to the pond. It must be cut over every three or four years if we want to see the migrating waterfowl on most of the pond.

This area of brush stretches from the north line to the south and is about a hundred feet wide. The south line area is a tangled mass and is difficult to manage thus it is slowly heading into the pole timber category.

The vegetation in this brush area consists of seedlings and small trees of hawthorn, cherry, juneberry, apple, red maple, poplar, tulip poplar and willow. Two autumn olive trees which were received from the Game Commission were planted in this area. They have now joined the list of nuisances and are difficult to control since their seedlings pop up almost everywhere. However, the willow still dominates this area and creeps into my roads and paths making them impassable, if not cut back.

This brush area slopes to the pond and all water run off from the house and several seeps work their way toward the pond. making some portions of this brush area permanently wet. It is little wonder that the willows thrive.

Generally I start clearing the brush on the left facing east and the pond and clear back toward the right. I clear about a hundred feet each year. By the time I get to the right side five years have elapsed. That is why the right area, that is along the south line, has grown up to pole timber. The fact that I wish to keep the view open also causes me to neglect that south brush area, but it does not interfere with the pond view.

In among the small trees are clematis vines and multiflora rose, which are also nuisances. Some field guides said that the rose hips are "relished" by birds and other creatures. If this were true then why are the rose hips still on the twigs in mid-winter? I agree that animals eat rose hips but I wouldn't use the word relished, perhaps necessity is a better term.

Since I cut this area back the apple trees never reach maturity. However, their bark is eaten by rabbits and when I cut the apple and hawthorn trees I make a special high pile of them so rabbits can have them for emergency food when the snow starts falling. Their tracks are often seen around and leading into brush piles.

Interspersed in this brush area are a few high bush plants as well as various grasses and some goldenrod. There are two large blueberry bushes, about four feet high, which produce an abundant crop each season. The wild berries are harvested by critters just before they are ripe enough for me. I occasionally do get a couple of handfuls of berries when the birds have not completed their stripping.   The nesting birds in this brush include the willow flycatcher, least flycatcher, chipping sparrow and catbird. A large maple overlooks the area and it is a nesting place for the northern oriole. At the edge of a section of this brush there are four large hawthorn trees. These trees provide fruit as well as a nesting place for the goldfinch, catbird and yellowthroat warbler.

The willows grow at a rapid rate. They send up long shoots from a central cluster. The outside shoots become top heavy and bend toward the earth. They often lay on the ground. This ground limb then sends down roots and an upright limb, which becomes a new trunk. It becomes a runner of roots and shoots. Thus, the willow can creep from one place to another almost undetected. When cutting back the willow the new trunk lying horizontal on the ground is often overlooked and the willow is quickly back in business.

Roadside

There is another large brush section between Elgin Road and the house-mowed area. This area is five hundred feet long as it borders the road and is about fifty feet wide. It is home to goldenrod, blackberry, and red raspberry as well as tree seedlings of the various types previously mentioned. There is a twenty-foot square patch of milkweed that receives special attention. When the milkweed pods are about an inch long I eat them raw and enjoy their nutlike flavor.

This area is also a wild butterfly garden that is visited by monarchs, yellow swallowtail, black swallowtail, viceroy, red admiral, fritillary, sulfur and cabbage butterflies. Sometime in June I begin checking the milkweed leaves for the black and yellow, with a tinge of green, larva of the Monarch butterfly. Later I look for the chrysalis, which is where the larva transforms into a butterfly. The moth transformation is carried on in a cocoon.

A second butterfly garden is a twenty by twenty eight foot wild flower garden that I constructed on the west side of the house. I transplanted specimens of most all the wild flowers I could find in the local area. About half the species did not survive the competition but those that did attract a variety of insects including wasps, bees and butterflies. The bee balm and dames rocket have done very well as transplants while the goldenrod, chicory, evening primrose, yarrow and curled dock need constant thinning.

In the roadside brush area there are sumac, multiflora rose, chokecherry, pine, and on the southern end are apple, hawthorn with sumac. I let two apple trees mature. They are centerpieces among the brush. These trees produce an abundant crop of apples most years and I have many woodchucks as well as deer feeding on them. The wind carries seeds from the trees on the other side of Elgin Road to our brush area. This property, across the road, is owned by two elderly ladies who reside permanently in Florida. It is part of an estate that probably will never be occupied or sold. It has giant oak, tulip poplar, black cherry, red maples, Scotch Pine, white pine, and Norway Spruce on it. The property consists of more than a hundred acres with most of the trees on it at least a hundred years old. Some old roads can be identified in this forest as well as the remains of an old dwelling which appears on maps dated 1853.

It pains me to cut the seedlings that sprout in the brush area but it is essential that I keep this area in in brush if I am to maintain different habitats. I have transplanted several spruce and tulip poplar seedlings into the wet flatland brush.

The roadside brush contains large areas of blackberries, red raspberries and a few black raspberry bushes. The red raspberry is more plentiful than the black, which is unfortunate since the black raspberry is my favorite berry. I have tried to propagate the black raspberry near my garden without success. I have been told that one cannot propagate black raspberries if there are red raspberries in the vicinity.

When daughter April was about four years old, one evening she and I filled up her sailor hat with red raspberries. She immediately ran with them toward her grandma Irene who was and is her favorite person. April stumbled and the berries went flying into the cut grass. It was a pitiful sight to watch the little girl trying to find the berries. These were the last berries of that season which added to the small disaster.

Generally I leave the blackberries and raspberries for wildlife. In years of abundance, which has been common lately, I have made two blackberry pies a season. Last year I froze a quantity of wild blackberries mixed in with my low bush blueberries to make a pie for New Year's Day. Even though they flourish here the low bush blueberries were not originally on this property. They were dug up and transplanted from a field on the other side of Union City.

Least Weasel

There are many animals that are so secretive one may never know they exist. Such is the case of the least weasel and shrew which live in this roadside brush area. Our driveway passes through the center of this brush and some animal catches these small critters every year and places them on the driveway. I have never been able to identify the predator but believe it is a cat from one of the barns in the neighborhood. The nearest neighbor barn is seven hundred feet away.

The least weasel (*Mustela nivalis)* is one of the smallest carnivores in the world. It has teeth like tiny thorns and a body the size of a mouse. It lives in a miniature jungle, living by tooth and claw. It is a hunter that is hunted by larger predators including snakes, larger weasels, bobcats and, of course, house cats. The least weasel is a rare animal and we are fortunate to have them here at Hawk's Nest. Even though it is not common, it can be found as far south as the Carolinas and as far north as Alaska.

The least weasel has the typical body build of its larger relatives. This includes a long neck and short tail. The male is about eight inches in length with three inches being tail. The female is slightly smaller. They only weigh about two ounces.

The diet of the least weasel is believed to be mostly mice, shrews, and ground nesting birds. They may also eat insects since that is a common food for animals of that size.

31

The least weasel is a beautiful brown on top and white below. Some are believed to take on a white phase in winter. The term rare may be misused since these are so secretive it is very difficult to determine their exact numbers in a given area.

Shrew

We have a variety of shrews that live in the patch of roadside brush. Identification has been made on the carcasses found on the driveway as well as shrews brought to the house by our house cats before we decided to keep them confined to house. .

We had two kittens dropped off on Elgin Road and they wandered down to our house. Who can resist kittens? We named them Pandora and Luna and had them spayed. They were wildlife hunters. Whenever we let the cats out we confined Bear Dog in his digs for the period of time the cats were loose. One day Luna disappeared and we put an ad in the paper for her recovery. This was before we decided to confine our cats to the indoors. A couple of months after her disappearance Bear Dog brought the remains of Luna to the house. Later son Matthew brought home a kitten which he named Abigail and she joined Pandy as our second cat. Anyway let us return to the shrews.

I have turned up ground nests, which I initially believed to be mouse nests at one time. They were probably shrew nests. They were balls of leaves and dried grass with a peculiar odor about them that is different from the odor of mouse. Our sense of smell is one of the most accurate senses we have and once we have identified and recorded an odor in our memory it becomes part of our mental inventory. Perfume manufacturers know this and make their fortunes by this fact.

Shrews as a group are among the most populous animals on earth and yet most people have never seen one and most of those who have seen one probably think that they have seen a mouse. A handy classification of shrews is short-tailed and long.tailed with the latter being the most abundant.

There are seven species of shrews found in Pennsylvania. Five of them have identified at Hawk's Nest. Different shrews that have been observed here are the masked, pygmy, short-tailed and least, the latter two being in the sort-tailed category.

All shrews have velvet-textured fur, very small eyes, hidden ears, and a pointed snout. Their nostrils open to the side.

Shrews feed mostly on insects and sometimes plant material. They eat earthworms, snails, spiders, and will kill and eat mice. They move above and below the ground, mostly utilizing mole trails when underground.

Shrews are a unique animal in that they possess poisonous saliva. The poison was observed to affect mice in laboratory experiments by lowering blood pressure, which was followed by paralysis and death. In nature the shrews poison is diluted and does not have the potency of the lab situation. However, if the poison has time to act it will subdue a mouse.

Shrews are quite small. The largest shrew, which is the short-tailed shrew *(Blarino brevicaudo)* is four and one half inches long and weighs a half-ounce. Most other shrews are just over two inches long in body with a tail adding perhaps another inch and a half.

A third area of the brush on the tract is along the north property line and could be considered a hedgerow. Here are mature apple trees surrounded by blackberry on the hill and willow in the small valley. Poplar trees spring up every year and are cut back when they reach ten feet. It is best to cut back the poplar as soon as it emerges because of its habit of sending out runner roots that spring into full-blown trees in a very short period of time.

Here in the fence line hedgerow is the catbird and its nest. It can be seen darting in and out of the shrubbery making its squeaky cat-like sound. Shortly after raising its young the catbird takes off for Central America.

At Hawk's Nest the catbird feeds on ants, beetles, grasshoppers and caterpillars. After I open up the top of an ant mound I often observe the gray catbird flitting in and out of nearby shrubbery waiting for me to leave..

Another bird that has been coming back to this hedgerow each year is the brown thrasher. It lives in the large brush area down from the house. I have never found a thrasher nest and I have never seen more than one at a time. I have never seen young brown thrashers on the property. I have been told that the brown thrasher mates for life and if the mate perishes the surviving spouse lives a solitary life. Perhaps that is some sort of wishful sentimental thinking.

The hedgerow brush areas are where we find vines such as clematis, Virginia creeper, wild grape and greenbrier. We also have a patch of poison ivy in the vicinity of the wood swamp, a very wet place in the lowland forest area.

Woodcock (*Scolopak mino*)

For the first couple of years at Hawk's Nest I would see nail-like holes in wet mud along the trails. I recognized these as the telltale signs of the woodcock also known as the timber doodle. Eventually I began flushing out woodcock and as always felt a kinship with this long-billed, bulky bird with the close-set eyes. It is a shore bird adapted to the uplands..

The woodcock lives in shrubbery and on abandoned farmland that is going back to nature. It prefers open woodland and low cover.

I finally discovered a woodcock nest at the edge of the area on the north property line. It was unfortunate since I stepped on the female and cracked the three brown and white eggs that were under her. The situation would not have occurred had the bird flushed out. When I stepped on her there was no sound and she made a short hop, which caught my eye, and then I was aware of what had happened. The female didn't move after its hop and I walked away. The next day I checked the eggs and certified that they were cracked. The woodcock was no longer evident.

For the rest of the summer I was haunted by the sight of the woodcock huddled beside the nest of cracked eggs. Even as I write this the scene is etched in my mind. Somehow situations as this have to be accepted as a part of nature or else one will be bogged down in guilt and wishful thinking. What fate was it that prevented my step from being four inches to the left or to the right?

A fourth area of brush exists on what I call the flats. It is about a half-acre dissected by a small stream which flows into Lilley Run. Here are blue beech, maple leaf viburnum, nannyberry, elderberry, small hemlocks, and some willow. Here is where deer bed down and here is their escape route into the swamp.

Here may be seen muskrats and beaver as they move between the pond and the creek. Cedar waxwing and rose-breasted grosbeak usually nest in this area.

The elderberry, bush honeysuckle, and nannyberry add interest to the foliage close to the pond. There is also a clump of pokeweed that provides food for our bluebirds, rose-breasted grosbeak, blue jays, mourning dove, cedar waxwing, catbird, and cardinal. Opossum and raccoons also eat the pokeweed fruits and it is common to find raccoon skat in autumn with a tinge of blue in it.

White nannyberry *(Viburnum lentago)* blossoms appear in late May and the black fruit ripens in late August. The fruit is a large flat seed encased in a sweet purple pulp. The plants provide enough fruit so that I don't have to compete with the animals and the birds that eat them. Deer browse on the twigs and rabbits gnaw at the trunks of the clumps of shoots which are characteristic of nannyberry. Most of these clumps are six feet high but there is one large clump that reaches a height of twelve feet.

Neighbor Jim is a volunteer with the State Game Commission. He is often called upon to trap beaver that are causing flood or tree damage. Usually he brings the beaver to Hawk's Nest and releases them in the flats. In this location they have a choice of moving to swamp, stream or pond.

Beaver as it emerged from Jim's cage.

Juneberry *(Amelanchier species)*

When people drive by a wooded area in spring and see trees loaded with white blossoms they are apt to think that these are dogwood or apple but not many will think of juneberry, also known as shadbush and serviceberry. The different names are associated with different aspects of the tree.

It is juneberry in our area because the red fruits ripen in that month, shadbush in southeastern Pennsylvania because that's when the shad run up from the ocean and Sarvis berry in West Virginia when this was the first wild fruit in spring that fed the early pioneers.

The junebrry is a small tree and a vital part of our shrub and brush areas. I transplanted four along the driveway fifteen years ago. One of them didn't survive. Those that did survive are beautiful. They are loaded with white blossoms each spring and produce an abundance of fruit in late June and early July. Their trunks are eight inches in diameter and their height is twenty seven feet.

Just about any animal or bird that eats fruit dines on the juneberry. We eat them by the handfuls. They taste somewhat like fermented plum. Some people do not like the seeds which make up a third of the bulk of the quarter inch fruit. However, these chew easily and I find it adds to the interest of their consumption. .

One of the three juneberry trees that survived along the driveway is a favorite of the yellow-bellied sapsucker whose neat holes occupy five upward feet of bark. This concerns me since the sapsucker already killed off the top of the only white birch tree at Hawk's Nest.

One of the surprises of the sapsucker event with the white birch occurred one evening as Bonnie and I were observing the insects buzzing around the oozing holes in the tree when a half dozen hummingbirds appeared and began draining sap from the oozing holes and eating insects that were attracted to the sap.

These were, of course, ruby throated hummingbirds, *(Archiloheus colubris)*. For some reason my mind could not accept the hummingbird as an insect eater. We had only connected them to our bee balm, jewelweed, and other flowers that are observable from our decks. Of course, we have deck flowers purposely planted to attract hummingbirds.

We usually put flowers in the deck planters to attract the three Bs- birds, butterflies, bumble bees. Often we are treated to a hummingbird dance where the hummingbird starts to move in a harmonic motion. These are short arc movements that are also described as pendulum movement. It is as if the hummingbird was performing for us and thanking us for the bounty we have provided.

All brush areas have juneberry in them. There are several tall juneberry trees in the deep woods just below the Middle Trail. However, the bigger trees of climax species are crowding these out.

There is a restaurant on the outskirts of Erie that has several juneberry bushes planted as ornamental shrubs. I discovered these one early July after dining in the restaurant. The fruit was ripe and I helped myself to them. This attracted the attention of the restaurant patrons who began staring at me. I decided to move on.

This incident reminded me of the time that I was walking along a street in the town of Warren and noticed a hedge of barberry loaded with fruit. Barberry is not an outstanding edible but these were interesting so I chewed the fruit and studied the plants. Barberry is notorious as an intermediate host for wheat rust. After about fifteen minutes a police car pulled up and an officer asked me what I was doing. The property owner had called them. I had a lot of explaining to do and did. In reference to this adventure my buddy Ron Boone said that in such instances it has been his experience that it is easier to beg forgiveness than to get permission.

POLE TIMBER

If a plowed field is abandoned in this area, seedlings of black cherry, hawthorn, red maple, sumac, and poplar will take root. In three years the seedlings will be three feet high and in ten years, twelve feet high. When they reach a diameter of four to ten inches they are considered pole timber, which may be defined as members of an immature forest. If undisturbed the pole timber eventually turns into mature forest. .

The seedlings are many and it is impossible for them all to survive to maturity. There may be as many as a hundred seedlings in an area ten by ten feet. Eventually they whittle down to twenty and eventually three or four when they reach three inches in diameter. A section of pole timber stands on the north line at the edge of the forest.

Another section of pole timber is on the south border along the fence with Farmer Al. There are pole timber sized trees in the forest and in the hedgerow but in these sections they are isolated and not clustered. The south fence line has apple, black cherry, and red maple interspersed with witch hazel, willow and elm. The north fence line has mostly poplar surrounded by wild apple, june berry and a few hemlocks.

I remember the hemlocks in this area well because I went to cut one out a few years ago and a horde of yellow jackets came out from a nest at its roots. I was on my knees with ax in hand and was not able to rise fast enough to escape. It was the first time I had a reaction to bee or wasp stings. I took an antihistamine, which helped the situation, but I still felt sick for hours.

The poplar trees on the north line are six to twelve inches in diameter and thirty feet tall. There are at least sixty trees in this section at this writing. Each year one or two trees succumb to crowding and die. These dead trees are worked over by the pileated woodpecker and its oblong holes look like yawning mouths on the sides of the trees. The silver white bark is reminiscent of the birch forests of northern Russia. Here is a beautiful sight as the setting sun casts its closing rays on the limbless white trunks. The tops of these trees are in stiff competition for sunlight.

Pileated Woodpecker

We have seen the pileated woodpecker (*Dryocous pileatus*) in every month of the year. It is the bird that hooked me on bird watching many years ago.

The pileated woodpecker is seventeen to nineteen inches long. It is spectacular with its red crest, its black and white feathers, and its heavy drilling bill. It flies with an undulating movement created by its quick wing beats and sudden pauses.

The pileated, like other woodpeckers, uses its stiff tail to brace itself as it moves up a tree. Its oblong deep holes pecked into dead trees are its calling card. These holes offer refuge to smaller birds in inclement weather.

The call of the pileated is a kuk-kuk, sometimes described as a kack-kack or a puck-puck. Once heard, the call is easily remembered.

The pileated will eat berries and nuts as well as the larva it seeks in dead trees. One was once seen on one of the ant mounds in our open field.

The apple trees in this pole timber section usually produce an abundant crop as do the juneberry, probably because they are more like individual trees and are not pressed by their neighbors. I have spent many hours trimming the apple trees on the property and many hours in this section. I also asked my neighbor Jim for permission to trim the trees on his property that border mine. He readily agreed and those trees also produce an abundant crop of apples each year.

Even though these apples came from the same stock there is a difference in texture, color, and taste in most of the dozen trees. A tree with one of the better tasting apples was blown down by a strong wind after it had leafed out in the spring of the year. The tree was on the fringe of the mini-forest. Its shallow root system added to its vulnerability. It was cut it up for firewood.

This section also has grapevines as well as some deep carpets of moss. Ruffed grouse as well as ring-necked pheasants have been observed in the vines. The grouse are native, but the pheasants are released each year by the Game Commission. They usually release six pheasants and in the thirty years we have been here none of them survived a year. One female pheasant came up to our winter feeder and it was still around in May, but it too met its demise.

Deer feed near the swamp and retreat to the area along Jim's fence line. His children maintain two tree stands and often "harvest" a deer. One snowy hunting season I came upon Jim's daughter Debbie dragging a buck out along our tractor road. The deer probably weighed more than she did. We talked for a while. She had gutted and field dressed the deer before starting the drag.

The south border pole timber area does not have the neat look of the straight poplars of the north. The upper limbs of hawthorn, black cherry, and red maple intertwine with a few poplars in the mix. This is where the hawks usually land as they survey the landscape and our bird feeders in winter. We often view them with field glasses from our dining room. They perch on the limbs and almost blend in. They swoop quickly to our feeders and often scoop up a junco or a chickadee. There were many hawks one year and we dubbed our feeders "hawk feeders."

The winter hawk species observed include Coopers, Sharp-shinned, Northern Harrier and Red-tailed. In summer, they are joined by the Red-shouldered Hawk and we have also seen some Peregrine Falcons and many Kestrels.

I like to visit this section of pole timber and have constructed two large brush piles in it. One brush pile is about twenty feet in diameter and seven feet high at this writing. The brush will decompose and flatten down over the years. This large brush pile must be fed and maintained, if is to survive as a wildlife sanctuary.

Another reason to visit this area is to stand in a great circle which was created near one edge of it. The circle is devoid of brush and is twenty-four feet in diameter. It would be a good place to hold nature rituals. If there are such things as faeries and little folk, they meet here.

There is another large circle between the barn and the main road. When seedlings of Scotch Pine took hold in the brush area near the road about a dozen of them were moved near the barn and placed a twelve-foot circle. Matthew was about two years old when I planted them and I wondered if he would discover the unique circular nature and perhaps set up a military camp and play soldier which seems to be the activity of every growing boy. He did discover the circle and mentioned it to me when he was thirteen years old. He and grandson Eli did play soldier outdoors as anticipated but they ignored this area. Their forays in their war against imaginary enemies took place in the deep woods.

Building outdoor shacks and shelters was a popular pastime in my youth. Every summer we would take to the hill and clean out a section of closely packed hawthorn bushes which we called haws and jagger bushes. We held our meetings within the confines of our thorny forts. Rival groups also built forts and we passed the summer looking for the other forts and destroying them. Eventually we outgrew the shack building mania and were old enough to get summer jobs.

There is a follow up to the shacks among the haws. One evening after my college classes I showered and noticed a small lump on my leg and a black splinter beneath the skin. When I dug it out it with a needle it was a haw thorn that had been in there at least six or seven years. Close examination revealed five more black lines, which I dug out. They had not festered and were simply embedded under the skin. Perhaps there are more that I have not yet discovered.

White-tailed Deer

The white-tailed deer (Odocoileus virginianus) at Hawk's Nest live in the thickets around the swamp. They often bed down in the fields at night and where they have bedded is obvious by the flattened grass. Many deer also hide in the pole timber thickets during the day.

White tailed deer paw through the snow below our kitchen window.

The deer travel back and forth in our two-mile valley, only moving out when some additional pressure is put on them, such as pursuit by dogs. We who live in the valley created by Lilley Run are all observers of nature and we discuss the deer and their physical characteristics of size, color, rack, and sex. We generally know the deer well by the end of summer and could probably give them names if we wished to do so.

In winter the female deer gather together in our Cathedral area and stomp the snow into a yard. When they move out to feed and when the snow is deep the largest doe will lead the way, breaking a trail for the others. They usually head for the hawthorn thicket or the apple trees where the branches are low enough to reach. When the leading doe stops moving a second large doe will take over the lead. Often the snow is eighteen inches deep and this is a strenuous exercise for the deer since it is almost chest high.

We watch them through binoculars as they break trail through the snow and make their way to the apple trees that are closer to the house than the hawthorn thicket. It is in the apple tree area that we used to put out food for them. We no longer do that and let nature take its course, but somehow in their memory they feel our food will still be there..

Each year I would buy a hunting license to support the Game Commission land acquisition program. There was some letters to my newspaper column questioning why I never wrote about my deer hunts. My discussions of deer hunting were quoting expert hunters, such as Jerry and Jim .

There came a time when I felt I should shoot a buck and certify myself as a true hunter. I had participated in cutting and processing deer several times in the past. And I certainly have enjoyed dining on venison.

Everett had purchased a 30-30 rifle and I thought about using it. After a discussion with Trapper Jim I decided to use a twenty gauge shotgun with a slug or punkin ball. On the first day of buck season I positioned myself at a cross trail section of the pole timber where it merged with the brush. I thought about the eighty pounds of clean meat and storage of it and the fact that only Everett and I would eat it. My thoughts went along like that as several does wandered by

Eventually, a six point buck came within twenty yards of me. Why kill a deer? What purpose would it serve? My deer hunting friends are always offering me part of their kill so I didn't need the meat. I whistled and the buck leaped sideways and moved quickly out of sight.

Shooting something is not a sport. The sport and enjoyment is in the hunt. I had enjoyed the hunt and the satisfaction of knowing I was able to kill a deer if I ever had a reason or need to do so.

Unfortunately for most deer they follow their trails and those that we have made. This makes them vulnerable to a hunter waiting along the trail.

The pregnant doe drop their fawns in June and there is always excitement when we stumble across a fawn hiding along the trails. When we find a fawn we know it has not been abandoned and if we move off to an observation point, as we have often done, we will see the mother return and the fawn rise and suckle.

One time Irene came up from the swamp and said she saw a huge brown and white snake in the tall grass of the swamp. When Bonnie and I followed her directions we found a newly born fawn with its speckled coat lying motionless about two feet from the trail.

This fawn was hiding in the grass on the edge of the swamp. It is evident in this black and white photo, but it was hardly noticeable in the real environment.

It was one sunny day in early autumn when I walked on the Middle Trail and a doe came running straight at me at full speed. I stepped to the side as she raced by followed quickly by a buck that also ignored my presence. Just as I started on the trail again, here came another buck also at break neck speed. It was the breeding season and I was in their way.

Even if we never saw a deer we would know they are here from the buck rubs on small saplings, bucks scrapes and the browse line on trees. A buck scrape is an area where the buck marks territory by pawing the earth and urinating on it.

Buck rubs on small saplings appear in rutting season.

We hear deer snorts, whines, and whistles coming out of the brush. We see the twig ends of our small apple trees chewed back each year. We see deer bedding areas. In winter we follow their tracks in the snow and in summer we find their tracks in the clay on the trails. Their split hoof prints are everywhere and we can trace their movements along their well worn trails.

After one hunting season there was a large buck lying dead in the grassland near the south fence. It had apparently been wounded and made it to the grassland before it perished. It was a good chance to watch nature take its course in disposition of a carcass. It was easily observed by walking thirty feet from a path out from the swamp. Jerry had mentioned the eight.point rack and said he would take it. He never did.

On one occasion there were six turkey vultures sitting in a dead tree near the carcass. They obviously were pecking at it. The odor was strong at the time of the buzzards.

The carcass was still there when the snow began to fall in earnest in late November. There were many fox tracks around the dead deer. Trapper Jim asked if he could set traps for them. He set two traps but was never successful in getting a fox.

What was obvious was that both Jerry and Jim were constantly moving through the woods and fields of the valley. Their visits were observed me, or by members of our household.

When we first met Jerry he often gave us deer meat. Eventually Jerry said he found deer hunting no longer a sport or exciting with a rifle so he took to archery and still harvested a buck every season. He became. so proficient in archery he entered a contest in Michigan and hit a regular paper plate at a hundred yards and won a Polaris four wheeler complete with a cart. There were some legal battles between the contest organizers and the Polaris Company as to which one should award the prizes. Apparently they never thought anyone would be able to hit that elusive a target. Jerry did get the four wheeler and took me on a bumpy ride deep into the brush railroad bed to see a ring of large mushrooms he had discovered in a hawthorn thicket. I never wanted another ride on that vehicle even though I did get some great photos of the "fairy" ring, which was fifteen feet in diameter. My attempts to identify the mushroom species were without success. They were medium brown in color and four inches high, closely clustered together as the ring was formed. Naturally, there are several photographs of this phenomena in my files.

Eventually Jerry quit archery and began hunting deer with a revolver. Of course, he was successful. Finally he gave up hunting deer until his grandson was old enough to hunt.

Jerry's affection for deer caused him to get legal papers permitting him to raise them. He fenced off a half acre of his property and purchased a large buck from a dealer. One day, while the family was away, dogs appeared at the enclosure and chased the deer in circles inside the fence while the dogs ran on the outside. The deer died. Some children saw the dogs from their school bus and reported them to Jerry. He eventually found the owners who paid the cost of the deer. Since then, Jerry has fenced in an acre and a half and has raised many deer.

Trapper Jim also got a deer every year. One season he was setting out muskrat traps on Lilley Run. He carried his deer rifle along, "just in case." Sure enough a buck approached him head on while he was setting a trap. It was an easy kill.

There was a twelve point buck reported in the area one year and I did see it out of our upper floor window as it made its way across the property. It was "harvested" on the first day of the buck season. Other deer incidents involved Farmer Al's fence. When Al raised cattle he was proud of his Ryan Fence which was four feet high with four-inch square wire openings. One section of this fence was between our properties. Large deer could leap this with ease, but not the young yearlings. One morning I found a doe hanging on the fence by a hind leg. I freed her and she limped off. When the doe tried to leap the fence her back leg came down in a top square and the foot was entwined in the wire.

A few weeks ago there was another similar incident. When I released Bear dog from his pen he ran to the site and it was only then that I noticed the deer hanging there. Bear started attacking its head. I took Bear back to his pen and went to free the deer. Its leg was broken and when it was finally free it could barely drag itself away. Later in the afternoon I found it dead about thirty feet from the site. I dragged it deeper into Al's field. About a week later the entire carcass was gone except for a small square of hide and the head. Perhaps, it was taken by a black bear.

There are coyotes in the area, but I don't believe they could have moved the entire carcass. When we camped on the property before the cabin was built we saw several coyotes, but have not seen them since that time. Their scat indicates that they are here.

My observation of deer chewed twigs indicates a heavy leaning toward maple, apple and hemlock. Other plants browsed were willow, wild black cherry, sumac, and poplar. Low plants were the ferns, blackberry and goldenrod. I suppose they will eat whatever leaves and twigs are available at any particular time of year. There is no shortage of browse here, so hunters in in the area find no shortage of deer.

One year a particularly large buck appeared down by the cabin. I got out the video camera and recorded about ten minutes of him. When I mentioned the buck to Jim he said a lot of hunters already had their eye on him. Jim was also a volunteer deputy warden for the Game Commission and had many opportunities to talk to hunters in his line of work.

On the Monday after the opening day of buck season which was the previous Saturday, the *Corry Journal* reported that a man who lived over the ridge from us had "harvested" one of the biggest bucks every seen in the area. The case was closed.

We keep a salt block out all year and do not permit hunting on our property although violation of this policy is so rampant that our family members stay near the house during the two weeks of the regular deer season. The salt block is easily seen from the dining room window. It is slightly over a hundred feet from the house. The deer visit it almost every evening.

Once there were porcupine tracks in the snow at the block. The block location is a fair distance from the porcupine habitat so the animal can not afford to be a frequent visitor to the block. It would be easily caught by its deadly enemy, the bob cat.

Studies by the Pennsylvania Game Commission indicate that a forest will support five deer per square mile while swamp area will support up to twenty deer per square mile. Hunters who own property for the purpose of hunting deer would do well to keep their land in brush if they want a continuous supply of deer.

Once Bonnie and I stopped to sit on one of the benches overlooking the swamp along our south line. We have benches scattered over the property. We sat for about twenty minutes and observed a Great Blue Heron moving from pool to pool. When we got up to leave, a huge doe leaped to its feet and ran through the swamp. It had been lying on a grassy spot less than ten feet from us which indicates something about our powers of observation or maybe something about the deer. I suspect many hikers walk past deer lying low and never know they are there.

In one Game Commission experiment there were four tagged deer in a ten-acre enclosure. The Commission wanted to get rid of the deer to start another project so they permitted six hunters to enter the enclosure and kill the deer. The six hunters walked the ten acres for more than ten hours and never saw the deer. The deer were later traced with electronic equipment and shot. This supports my assumption that many hunters will walk by a hiding deer and never see it.

OUR FOREST

Hawk's Nest is located in the Northern Evergreen Forest region which stretches from Minnesota east to Maine and from southeastern Canada south around the Great Lakes and to central Pennsylvania. The climax forest trees are beech, maple and hemlock. We are less than an hour's drive to the Central Hardwoods where the forest is dominated by oaks and maples.

George Petrides in his book *A Field Guide to Trees and Shrubs* lists our forest type as "Lake Forest," which is one name for the forest of the Great Lakes region. The true Northern Evergreen Forest of Canada and Northeast United States has more pine in it and less hemlock than we have here.

Logging is a principal endeavor in the area with at least twenty sawmills within thirty miles of our property. Timber speculators who want to buy the rights to harvest our timber constantly visit us. We have been told that some of our wild black cherry trees are worth more than three thousand dollars each with two probably worth five thousand. These prime trees are used for veneering. Some of the local cherry tree trunks are sold in Germany and some in Japan. So far, we have chosen not to sell our timber. Both properties on either side of us and across the old railroad bed have been selectively cut since we have moved here.

Our forest, like every other forest, provides great benefits to our world. The use of wood for fuel is most apparent as many families in our immediate area have smoke rising from their chimneys in the winter. We augment our electric heat by using a wood burning furnace. We usually burn about four cords in a cold winter and three cords in a mild winter. The first winter we lived in the house we burned eight cords. It was one of the coldest winters ever recorded in the area. The record low according to my recording thermometer was exactly thirty degrees below zero Fahrenheit. For the high one summer we hit a hundred degrees Fahrenheit. Our average temperature for the year is fifty two degrees Fahrenheit. With global warming and our recent mild winters we do not have a need for large amounts of firewood.

The local forests provide building materials. Large racks of rough cut lumber can be seen in three locations less than fifteen miles from here. A booming chair industry was part of the economy of Union City, just seven miles away. That industry went into decline with competition from less expensive furniture industries.

The forests provide scientific information as well as recreational use. The western border of the Allegheny National Forest (ANF) is less than forty miles from Hawk's Nest. There are hundreds of miles of hiking trails in the Allegheny National Forest as well as several well-developed and primitive campsites. We have often used those facilities. It is the only national forest to show a profit in management in the last sixty years. Its chief timber product is the wild black cherry tree, which is in demand in construction as well as in furniture.

Maintaining forests also aid in flood control. Almost one hundred percent of the rain that falls in a forest is retained within the forest and returned slowly to the major creeks leaving it. When the large forests of the Pacific Northwest were first cut, towns like Astoria, Oregon were damaged by flooding.

The best use of the forest at Hawk's Nest is its use for wildlife Almost every wild mammal found in Pennsylvania has been identified on this property. The only major Pennsylvania mammals not seen here are the thirteen lined ground squirrel, snowshoe hare, ermine, some species of bats, and the recently introduced elk.

My idea of tending the forest is not to change the forest but to keep it operating as a viable ecosystem. This is my purpose for all the habitats at Hawk's Nest.

Those pioneers who were the first to clear the forest for farming and grazing land are to be commended for their efforts. However, today the value of forests must be balanced against the need for commercial development. It may be a good thing that many nonproductive farms are going back into forests. The forests of Pennsylvania have been cut over five times since William Penn's days. Today, only small pockets of virgin forests exit in the state.

If we abandon a plowed field it will quickly revert to grasses, low succulent plants, rushes, reeds and flowers. Within two to three years small trees will appear and within a short time they will be ten feet tall. In twenty years these will be pole timber followed by open woods and after thirty years the climax forest is well on its way to development.

In our forest there are hemlock trees that are at least a hundred years old. One that was blown over was cut and the growth rings indicated an approximate age of 78 years. Another hemlock tree indicated an age of 110 years. Our largest sugar maple is probably two hundred years old.

According to my circumference measurements when I compared our trees to those cut nearby some wild black cherry trees are over a hundred years old. There is an ancient butternut tree on the property. We lived here for almost ten years before it was discovered. We also have a white ash with a seventeen-foot circumference measured five feet above ground level. Son Matthew and I measured its height by using trigonometry and arrived at a height of 105 feet. One maple measured 98 feet and the largest free growing poplars are slightly over eighty feet

As the field turns to forest the first trees to gain a foothold are aspen, wild cherry, apple and hawthorn. That is if the area is well drained. If it is wet then willow takes over, along with viburnum, red maple, and red-osier dogwood.

In our big woods, the cherry trees are strong and healthy and quite valuable. One time I had made a deal with a logging outfit to sell seventeen of the black cherry trees. The main man gave me nine hundred dollars front money. They were to arrive on a Monday and begin harvesting. When I checked the area on Sunday the logger had marked off over thirty trees. After many attempts at trying to reach the logger daughter April finally succeeded. She was very angry and told the man to come and pick up his front money. We found out later the man had a warrant out for his arrest. He probably intended to take the trees and I would never see him again. My friend Bruce said that loggers and used car salesmen were the crookedest rascals in our society.

The other dominant species in our forest are red sugar maple, yellow birch, hornbeam, gray beech, and hemlock. Minor tree species, that is minor in numbers, include white oak, red oak, tulip polar, elm, apple, white ash, and hickory.

Remnants of the early pioneer species can be seen as they die out and are replaced by the climax, shade tolerant species. Large poplars continue to die and their trunks are riddled with oblong pileated woodpecker holes and their bases gnawed by animals, especially porcupines. Large apple trees are almost forty feet high with fifteen-inch trunks. Most do not provide usable fruit since many of their limbs are dead. In a good year the limbs that are green will provide small green apples relished by many woodland creatures.

The hawthorns are also on their way out with the largest trunks about eight inches in diameter. Most are like dead posts standing in the woods. When grandson Eli was a child and we walked in the woods he delighted in pushing these trunks over with his walking stick.

Scattered throughout the woods are a few hickory nut trees whose fruits were not obvious for years since the squirrels, chipmunks, and other animals harvested them immediately. So far I only found one white oak tree on the property. It is like a post almost thirty feet tall. Wishing to preserve and enhance it I cleared out a twenty-foot area around it. There is danger in doing this with a slender tree since it grew that way to reach for the sun among competitor trees. It spent its energy resources on height and this weakens the trunk, which is easily broken. This is true of slender trees if the upper top is weighted by leaves or snow or buffeted by high winds. The white oak has a patch of bark missing from halfway up to the ground. Apparently it was a lightening strike.

About ten years ago I found a tulip tree growing among the elms and red maples along the trail. The tulip tree was twenty feet high and two inches in diameter. There are not many tulip trees in our forest. I removed the trees around it and within a week the tree bent over. I took a ladder and some rope to the site and tied it at a height of twelve feet to other trees. It was a mess of ropes but held the tree firm. I put chicken wire around the slender trunk to a height of six feet to discourage buck rubbing.

At this time the tulip tree has not increased much in height but its girth increased to four inches. The ropes are gone and it stands unaided. The chicken wire remains and has been repaired. Bernd Heinrich in his book *The Trees In My Forest,* refers to these tall skinny trees as "vine **trees.**"

The lower vegetation in the forest is tall brush dominated by witch hazel, wild grapes, some blue beech and gray beech saplings. The witch hazel often grows against and around other trees. Once I found a red maple about six inches in diameter completely surrounded by witch hazel. The maple eventually died and I was able to push it over since its roots could not compete with the strangle hold of the witch hazel which was a circle of shoots about fifteen feet high.

There is little browse for deer at ground level in the forest so the deer feed at the edges of the brush areas and feed in the forest only when the beechnuts have dropped. In winter they browse on the lower limbs of the hemlock and their browse line is obvious.

A dead tree creates an open spot in the forest canopy. Sunshine penetrating the canopy encourages the growth of blackberry, raspberry, gooseberry, spicebush, partridge berry, ferns, and ground pine.

There is competition for the beechnuts between deer, squirrels, porcupine, chipmunks, wild turkey and ruffed grouse. The white-breasted nuthatch seems to be in abundance when the nuts are ripe. Yellow-bellied sapsuckers drill holes in the bark of the beech then eat the insects found on the oozing sap. Many of the insects get trapped in the syrupy sap and helplessly await the sapsucker's visit.

One strong windstorm brought down a dozen large beech limbs. These were fifteen inches in diameter at their base and around thirty feet in length. We use three to four cords of firewood each winter to supplement our electric heat. This windfall filled the bill. Beech is an excellent producer of heat and is easily split with a maul.

Black Bear

Our valley is not large enough to support a black bear which requires forty square miles of forest habitat. It is a true resident of the forest although it wanders about in any location during breeding season or when it is searching for food. The Black Bear (*Ursis Americanus)* often pass through our woods and we have been lucky enough to see one. Other people walking in our woods have seen more bears than we have.

When a bear appears in the area, word quickly spreads in our valley community of five families. Irene was the the first of our household to see a bear and was so excited we couldn't determine what she was saying. We thought she had seen a Black dog that occasionally visited us. Eventually we all were able to see the bear standing tall in the brush.

There was a black bear raiding dog dishes in the town of Wattsburg· ten miles to the north. The bear was tranquilized by the Game Commission officers and relocated ninety miles into the Allegheny National Forest. Within two days the bear was back in Wattsburg. People stopped leaving food out for their pets and the bear eventually moved on.

Once the beech nuts start falling in our forest there is an influx of wild turkeys *(Meleagris gallopavo)* They scratch up the dead leaves searching for the nuts and their visits are easily identified. These scratchings continue into winter and resume when the snow has melted. We once counted sixty-three turkeys walking in a line on the pond road. There was ten inches of snow on the ground at that time.

Wild turkey is the bird from which all domestic turkeys have descended. It prefers to escape by running rather than flying. When they do fly it is like a bushel basket moving through the air.

One spring, when we were between dogs, a tom turkey appeared where we park our vehicles. It strutted around for a day and we left it alone. It was still there the next day. It had a beard about ten inches long. It would attack us as we went to our vehicles. Even though it was interesting to watch it became a threat to our peace of mind.

It began chasing our vehicles as we left the driveway. After it had been around for eight days it finally got side swiped by Everett's car as he left the driveway early in the morning. It didn't move and stayed at the edge of the brush in a huddled position. I went to examine it and it hopped slightly then collapsed. Nothing left to do but end its misery.

The rogue turkey that harassed us for days.

There were a few more attempts to get it on its feet but these failed. I took my 22 caliber revolver up to the road and shot the turkey in the head and carried it to the back yard. I was still not convinced that it was dead because of the small caliber of the weapon so I decided to decapitate it with the ax that was handy. As I swung the ax Matthew, who was six at the time, and a friend had just exited the school bus and came upon the scene. The friend said to Matt, "let's get out of here." I took the carcass and placed it down in the flats. It was completely torn apart and consumed within two days.

Our ruffed grouse *(Bonasa umbellus)* feed on beechnuts. tree buds, and especially wild grapes when they are in season. Often when I walk along the trails and pause it causes the huddled grouse to explode out into the woods. Probably if I kept on walking the grouse would stay huddled and I would not know it was there. How many grouse did I pass in my hurried evening walks?

I once saw two grouse under a few hemlock branches that I had recently made into a loose pile. I continued walking. When I gave Everett the location of the grouse he was able to see them. However, he always walked with our dog Lobo and she scared them up.

One of my thrills was to see four immature grouse resting in the bends of some low grapevines. My movement caused two of them to leave their perches and race along the ground. The other two hopped to different perches on the vines.

There was an incident one autumn when we heard a gunshot in the woods. When I went to investigate the area there was a hunter dressed in an expensive hunting outfit and a beautiful retriever dog snuffling about. Together they looked like a painting from the late nineteenth century when such hunting outfits and dogs were fashionable. I have never been one to challenge a person in our woods, especially one with a gun, but I let him know I was there and in his presence, which was enough to get him to move on. Later in the day I found a decapitated grouse head in that part of the woods. I am not certain what that was all about. I assume it had been the target of the shot we heard and the hunter had decapitated and stored it before I got there.

Grouse are a resident of our wilder deep woods. These beautiful birds are subject to periodic population booms. Some years we would never kick up one and a few years later they seem to be in abundance. In a forest such as ours they will eat the buds of aspen, hawthorn, poplar, black cherry and birch. In the thickets they eat ferns, witch hazel, dock, and blueberry. They will eat fruits such as apple if they don't have to go too far areas to get them.

Squirrel

Other denizens of our forest include the gray and red squirrel. They are found in the hickory nut, hemlock and beech areas. Their footprints are evident in the winter snow, which dispels rumors of hibernation.

Squirrels were abundant in early pioneer days as diary entries of that time testify. A bounty of three pence was paid per squirrel by the Colony of Pennsylvania in 1749. There were more than 640 thousand squirrels harvested at that time. Today the squirrel harvest in Pennsylvania exceeds that of any other game animal.

When we lived in the cabin there were several large gray squirrels visiting the bird feeder. There were many black squirrels which are variations of the gray. These blacks were around for three years then they simply disappeared. The gray squirrel *(Sciurus carolinensis)* often has red or brown hairs intermingled with the gray, which might be difficult in identification and separation from the smaller red. There is no problem if you see them side by side.

Squirrel food is synonymous with nuts but they do eat many other foods including mushrooms, viburnum berries, and maple fruits as well as the newly emerging buds of maples and elms.

The squirrel nest is easily seen once the tree leaves begin to drop. The nest is like a bushel of leaves high in a tree. One that fell with a tree one winter contained grasses, moss and loose bark as well as leaves and twigs.

The red squirrel *(Tamiasciurus hudsonicus)* is a resident in abundance here at Hawk's Nest. A stroll in our woods sets it to squeaking and shrilling. It chirps like a bird and one might look for a bird when it does so. The red squirrel is the watchman of the woods. It is half the size of a gray squirrel and stories about combats between the two are often fabrications. If the size of the red is not recognizable then one must look for the white fur surrounding its eye.

We delight in watching the red squirrel at our winter feeders. Often they tunnel through the deep snow to get from one area to another. I measured one of the tunnels at forty-five feet by pacing it off. When frightened the red keeps to the ground whereas their gray cousins immediately climb any brush and tree that is handy. The red lives in the outer edges of the forest habitat while the gray resides deeper in the woods.

One winter, about six years ago, the reds decided that our house would make a better shelter than the dead maple at the edge of the brush area. About a dozen of them could be seen at the feeders and in the dead maple near the feeders. Then one night we heard scratching in the soffit above our bedroom window, which is on the second floor. The soffit was perforated aluminum and used for decoration rather than for air circulation on that side of the house.

We decided to let the squirrels alone and let the drama play out. The nails holding one edge of the soffit had given way and the squirrels moved into the opening. We were not certain as to how many there were but there were, like I said, about a dozen at the feeder. When spring arrived and the snow melted we stopped supplying the feeders. Our winter birds and the squirrels moved out.

I had to get the big ladder and tear down one side of the soffit to get at the nests. I recovered three wheelbarrow loads of nesting material, which were mostly goldenrod stems with leaves in among them. The goldenrod is abundant about thirty feet from the house and around that particular feeder where most of them congregated.

There are five large pine trees, four Scotch and one White near the old cabin site. They now bear huge cones and red squirrels have been observed in their branches. We expect the squirrel population to increase in that area in the coming years. .

Chipmunk

The chipmunk *(Tamias striatu)* is another critter of our forests. I have seen them in other habitats although I thought it was odd when I did. It is basically a creature of open woodlands. Our chipmunk population is not as great as I have seen in other years, but there are always enough of them to catch our attention and create visual pleasure. They will migrate from the forest as far as the house. A few years ago I found one swimming desperately in a five gallon bucket half full of rain water. It was fighting for its life since it could not get any footing on the bottom of the bucket to leap to the rim. I dumped it out onto the grass. It lay there for a long time then slowly rose and walked toward the brush as I gave it some advice.

There are not many months to observe the chipmunk since it goes underground sometime in November. Its extensive trails and burrows may be thirty feet long. Here it sleeps away and emerges in late February if there is sunshine. They usually appear in March although I recorded one on February 28 one year. However, I didn't see it again until the end of March. There was a foot of snow on the ground that February and the chipmunk had apparently made a mistake. I have seen a new family of young appear from their burrows in the first week of June.

If you come upon the chipmunk and surprise it you may see it rise like the classic prairie dog. If frightened it will cheep and high-tail it to its burrow. In a couple of seconds it will peak out at you.

Chipmunks like its bigger relatives eat nuts, wild cherries, fungi, any berry, weed seeds and maple seeds. I have seen them eating may-apples. Actually they eat just about any fruit or seed.

Despite their cuteness, the chipmunk is a notorious killer of small snakes, salamanders and insects including butterflies. They are accused of limiting the song bird populations by fifty percent in our county. They climb trees to raid bird nests of eggs and young birds.

The chipmunk travels mostly by daylight and is the prey of snakes, hawks, bobcats, foxes, weasels, and house cats. When we used to let our cats roam outside it was not unusual for them to bring a chipmunk to the mowed area and toy with it in endless games, which usually ended in death to the chipmunk.

Fox

Foxes are difficult to see unless one is willing to put in long hours of observation. However, they are somewhat easily called in by those who are adept at such things. Their tracks are often observed in the snow of winter. I can recognize the fox prints but have trouble separating the red fox from the gray fox. Neighbor Trapper Jim can tell the difference and proves it by catching them. He and his friend Ernie once treated me to an hour discussion on foxes and trapping one autumn evening.

I have been fortunate to observe both foxes at Hawk's Nest. The red fox *(Vulpes vulpes)* is spectacular in its orange red coat, black leggings, white throat and flowing tail tipped in white. Old Red stays pretty close to home, ranging at most only four miles. No need to go very far since there is an abundance of fox food here including mice, chipmunks, squirrels, shrews, moles, voles, rabbits, birds, grasshoppers, beetles, cherries, berries, and apples, as well as feral house cats. In nature, the prey animal must win every race.

The gray fox *(Urocyon cinereoargenteus)* has been easier to see even though its color blends in with the brush and forest. Its unusual habit, which I have observed, is its ability to shinny up a tree. This is quite an accomplishment considering it has digging rather than climbing claws. My one observation of this ability occurred when Bear dog and I came upon one eating some carrion it had taken to the forest. It scooted up a hemlock and climbed to a limb about ten feet above the ground. I could have easily knocked it off with a rock but moved on and demanded a reluctant Bear dog to come with me. However, the dog found the remains of the rabbit and carried it back to his enclosure. There is one record of a gray fox on a tree limb about sixty feet above the ground.

The gray fox will eat the same foods as the Red. When berries are ripe I often find its scat on logs, loaded with purple wild cherry stones and wild berry seeds. Also I have found pokewecd berries in the mix. .

According to Trapper Jim the gray fox is not as cunning as the red. He based that statement on the ease with which the Gray foxes respond to mechanical and electrical callers. American fox hunters rely on these methods rather than riding to the hounds.

I have never been able to find a fox den on this property. One den that I attributed to fox, was inhabited by mink. They must have a den close to Hawk's Nest since they are around all seasons of the year and they stay in their neighborhood.. Perhaps they prefer the neighbor lands where there are no trails and no continuous hikers.

THE LIVING TREES

If the professionals who trace human history and origins are correct, and there is no reason to doubt them, then we are descended from forest dwelling humans. We can live in almost any environment on earth, but we feel most at home in the forest.

The life cycle of trees and the physiology of trees are fascinating studies. They are as complicated as animals.

When we see a child racing around the yard at play we usually do not think of muscles, blood circulation, food intake, breathing, waste elimination and growth. We admire the beauty of the child. So it is with trees and their structures and growth. We admire the beauty of a tree and get involved with its internal structures only when the tree is threatened and we wish to save it.

The tree, just like the child, begins as a seed created by sexual reproduction. An acorn is an embryo inside a shell and most other tree seeds are such. In the spring when it is warm enough and moisture is present, great changes begin to take place in the seed. It is a complicated process and how this apparently dormant life is awakened is one of life's mysteries that scientists are about to solve.

The stored fats and starch in the seed begin to change into soluble sugars. The stored proteins become compounds of amino acids. The sugars and amino acids move to the growing points. The encased embryo splits its shell and the parts adapt to gravity and light. Those parts, which will become roots, move downward and those to become stems and leaves move upward.

Wherever the seed has fallen becomes the tree's permanent location for the rest of its existence. Sometimes some person or animal will come along and move the seed or transplant the tree to another location. However, the tree will survive best in the location where the seed has been dropped since its parents have survived to maturity in that same location. The success of the parent trees proved that the location is a desirable habitat for that species.

. The young stem reaches skyward and the cambium or growth layer develops in the stem. The inner cells will become wood and the outer cells will become bark. The cambium layer has the ability to divide and reproduce the cells necessary for this differentiation. As the tree ages the old bark continues to slough off while the wood continues to accumulate and send the tree outward and upward. Inside the cambium there are a group of cells that act as pipes delivering materials from the roots to the leaves and from the leaves back to the roots. If one cuts a swath of bark away from the trunk of the tree these pipes are interrupted in their work and the tree above the cut dies.

The wood formed in spring is light and fluffy compared to wood formed in late summer. This difference accounts for the growth rings in trees. Wet years and dry years are recorded The dates of landslides, volcanic eruptions, glacier movement and excess atmospheric carbon dioxide are recorded in the tree's growth rings and these can be correlated to trees not involved in the event and hence an approximate date can be established for these events.

Wood consists mostly of cellulose and lignin with small quantities of fats, sugar, starch, tannin, resin and water. The root makes up ten percent of the mass of a tree. Large trees have root systems that would reach hundreds of miles if they were stretched out. The roots provide water and nutrients to the tree as well as anchoring it in the ground. The health of the tree is directly related to the condition of the root system.

Gas and water are constantly moving through the stomata, which are small openings in the leaves. These openings close and open depending on the atmospheric conditions surrounding the tree.

When air enters the stomata the carbon dioxide is extracted and is utilized by chloroplast cells to manufacture chlorophyll. The reaction is regulated by enzymes, which utilizes oxygen and hydrogen to form water and then to form sugar. This is photosynthesis. In this process excess oxygen is created and that is the reason we keep green plants in a sick room. The tropical rainforests are so proficient at producing oxygen that they are referred to as the "lungs of the earth."

The energy for the transformation processes is supplied by sunlight. Without sunlight this process ceases. There are many published studies on this subject. In our Hawk's Nest forest the most favorable temperature for the process of photosynthesis is 70 degrees Fahrenheit in a diffused light. In hot direct sunlight the process is diminished. It is also essential to have an adequate supply of water, since the process is also slowed by a shortage of water.

All living things breathe in oxygen and give off water and carbon dioxide. Trees are living things. Living organisms need sugar for energy. We get sugar from the food we eat and trees get it by chemical changes. The process of photosynthesis is a reversal of the respiration process in trees. During the day trees conduct respiration and photosynthesis simultaneously. Photosynthesis ceases at night, but respiration continues in the entire tree including the cells of the bark, stem and roots.

A tree depends upon nitrogen for growth and it must get the nitrogen from the environment. Humans get nitrogen by eating plants. Nitrogen is added to the soil by decay processes. Lightning is reported to add seven pounds of nitrates per acre to the soil each year by its effect on atmospheric nitrogen, which is the most abundant gas in our atmosphere. Nitrogen is also added to the soil by nitrogen fixing bacteria. Soil fungi aid the trees in recovering vital nutrients such as nitrates, phosphates and potassium as well as trace elements.

Normal nitrogen must be transformed into nitrates for a tree to utilize it. This is a slow complicated chemical process. The locust tree has root nodules that can fix nitrogen and this gives it a genetic relationship to legumes such as peas. The seed pods of locust trees resemble pea pods adding to the evidence of the relationship.

My mother had what I thought was a strange superstition. She insisted on growing clover around our peach trees. I now know the relationship of clover to nitrogen fixing bacteria. My mother knew it worked but probably did not know why it worked. Another quirk she had was to get me to gather and bury leaves around the periphery of our fruit trees. By the time I realized her wisdom it was too late to tell her of my admiration of her insights.

There are other chemical elements besides nitrogen vital to a healthy tree. These include the traditional commercial fertilizers of potassium and phosphates as well as trace elements. It is now possible to introduce radioactive phosphorus or potassium into the soil and trace its daily movements throughout the tree.

As every gardener knows, water is the basic ingredient in all plant life as well as animal life. Sugars are made from carbon dioxide and water. Water is also a transportation system. It is absorbed by the roots and transferred to the leaves by the tree's internal water system.

The tree does not circulate water like a human circulates blood. The water moves from roots to the treetops. It does not fall back in the tree. A maple syrup producer told me the sap rises in the tree during daylight and falls back down at night, then rises the next day. This is not correct and to think about trees in those terms is misleading in understanding the internal working of the tree.

A tree can shut its stomata and prevent a loss of water. Sometimes there is confusion in the tree since it needs open stomata to get carbon dioxide for photosynthesis but it needs closed stomata to prevent water loss. Under hot conditions the tree closes its stomata and does not produce chlorophyll. This is why I previously mentioned our trees are healthiest at 70 degrees Fahrenheit on a thin cloud day.

Tree twigs, like most plants at Hawk's Nest, complete their growth by the end of June and start forming the bud tips for the coming year. However, growth of the trunk and stems continue laterally up until the time the leaves begin to fall. A warm week can cause the new buds to open prematurely, causing great harm to the tree. At the end of summer, the base of the leaf stem forms a fragile cell wall disconnecting it from its base.

Seeds are produced by fertilization of the female part of the flower. Seed production depends on the other activities of the tree. If the tree has rapid growth, as may be the situation in a competitive forest, then reproduction is diminished.

Trees grown in the open reproduce flowers and seeds much quicker than those that are crowded. The best apples and beech nuts are found in our meadow where a tree stands alone. In seed production a few weeks of dry weather and sunlight are good for flower pollination.

Trees, like every other living thing, grow old and die; It is best if living things grow old before they die. Sugar Maples and White Pines may live up to six hundred years. Some oaks have lived for fifteen hundred years. The oldest trees are the giant Sequoias or Redwoods, which may live to be forty five hundred years old. There is a Bristle Cone Pine in the Rockies that is believed to be the oldest living thing on earth.

The causes of tree deaths may be obvious, such as fire, flooding, drought or a lightning strike. Any damage to a tree invites fungus, disease and insects to attack. Many trees have a specific insect or fungus attacking it. Hence we get names like Pine Blister, Dutch Elm Disease, and Chestnut Blight. Some insects flourish best on a specific species of tree. These would include the gypsy moth seeking oak, apple and poplar and the tent caterpillar preferring wild black cherry or apple.

Like all living things, trees go through stages of life. They are an essential part of the environment. Our health and welfare depends in turn on the health and welfare of our trees.

Our woods fall under the class of "open woodland." When a tree such as the beech loses its limbs there is an immediate growth of blackberry and raspberry in the area of new sunlight penetration. Ordinarily the species on the forest floor are beech seedlings, prickly gooseberry, ground pine, spicebush, partridge berry, and flowers including trillium, wild leeks, and wood sorrel (oxalis) which grow in the moister areas.

Where trees have been removed witch hazel and blue beech .move in to join the blackberry and eventually eradicate it. One witch-hazel tree was six inches in diameter and twenty-five feet high. Of course it was in a clump of trunks with that one being the largest.

. The reproduction of most trees takes place when male pollen enters the female flower. This action usually takes place because of wind. One flower may produce several thousand grains of pollen and there are thousands of flowers on each mature tree. A person allergic to the pollen needs no reminder. When we walk through the woods during the high pollen season we breathe in thousands of these tiny grains with each inhalation.

The male and female parts are generally on the same flower in most tree species. A flower will reject its own pollen when pollen from another tree is available. Many studies have documented that situation.

Insects, especially bees that take pollen back to their nest also transport pollen back to other trees. When the bee lands on a new flower it still has some pollen in its hair and this fertilizes the female part of the flower. The bee relies on trees for its existence and in many instances the tree relies on the bee and other insects for its propagation.

Tree flowers appear before the leaves. If this did not occur the odds of wind blown pollination would be greatly reduced. Trees at Hawk's Nest that rely heavily on wind pollination are ash, elm, maples, beech, oak, birch, willow, and aspen.

Evolution in trees depends on cross-fertilization. If a tree pollinated itself then there would not be any genetic variation in the offspring. Trees propagated by cuttings are clones and do not participate in evolution. If there are hundreds of trees in an area and some catastrophe such as severe air pollution occurs it may be possible that some of the trees will be resistant to that pollution. When these survive and reproduce their offspring would most likely be resistant to that pollutant.

Most apples on a tree never make it to maturity since the tree regulates the number it can carry. In several trees at Hawk's Nest this process was not completed and the heavy weight of the fruit broke many limbs in two trees about a hundred feet from our dining room. Deer standing on their back legs and pulling down more limbs further damaged these trees. Eventually there was no recourse but to cut them down and use them for firewood. Apple wood burns nicely in a fireplace.

The woods at Hawk's Nest are strewn with glacial boulders. The falling leaves do not cover them since most protrude above ground level. Almost every one of these formerly bare rocks is covered with moss. When I gather boulders for decorative or building purposes I look for little mounds of moss because I know there will be a rock under it.

Mosses also grow on fallen trees and at the base of trees, usually on the north side of the tree. The ability to grow on the shady side of a tree trunk is due to the slower evaporation of moisture on that side away from the sun. Hence, in the northern forests, the moss at the base of a tree is a crude indicator of direction.

At the end of the Ridge Trail there is a small forest of club mosses generally called ground pine. They are about six inches high and look like miniature pine trees. These are lycopods whose ancestors were trees back in the Devonian and Carboniferous Periods.

The ground pine is found where the annual leaf cover is sparse which is on a slope where sunlight seeps through the deciduous trees. They move from one place to another by sending out a running branch. When this has grown about five inches long it will send down a root and send up a spike and begin another creeping branch. Over a period of years the ground pine moves from one area to another in this fashion.

Ground pine reproduces by yellow spores found on the tips of the upright shoots. These are highly flammable and were used as flash powder by photographers of old. They were also used as an ingredient of firecrackers.

The forest is a living environment. Much of the life in the forest is well hidden to one passing through. Those casual walkers only observe what happens to be before them at any given time. It is unlikely they will observe the interaction of insect life with the trees and with other creatures of the forest. The casual walker might see a cute chipmunk leap behind a tree but he will not observe this killer raiding a songbird nest of recently hatched young. It takes patient observation over a period of years to see that the spicebush, which was first discovered at the top of the hill, is no longer there but now flourishes on the slopes of the hill.

Horsetails grow along the old railroad bed, which has been cut through a section of Hawk's Nest. The cut bed is twelve feet below the eastern fence line. There is also a small area of horsetails growing in the soggy area below our sacred spring. These were used to scour soot from campfire pots when we camped and slept outdoors. Eventually we used an old oven grill for support and put aluminum foil under the pots to prevent the blackening.

Horsetails are descended from ancestors that lived over four hundred million years ago. Many of these ancestors were large trees then. I am told that horsetails are poisonous to cattle and horses but since I have never raised these animals I cannot verify that with first hand observations.

Trees in crowded woodland spend most of their energy rising high and competing for the sun. If they are going to survive they cannot afford to spend energy on growing side limbs and reproducing seed or fruit.

Hence, most deep forest trees have few lower branches. Most of the lower branches that the tree did produce are cut off from the main energy source and become dead limbs and eventually the tree casts them off. The hemlock tree is an exception to this limb casting procedure and the tree grows around them producing hard knots within..

At the tops of the competing trees there may be a lush growth of limbs and leaves. This may be hazardous to the tree when the first heavy snows rest on the tops, especially if the leaves have not begun to fall. The tree may topple or have its weak trunk break. This creates an open area in the forest and a new series of events take place.

Trees surrounding the new open space will send out limbs to get maximum sunlight. This puts the tree out of balance and it too may topple or break off. Thus, open spaces are created and the new sunlit ground will give rise to a host of plant species and the animals that use them.

Trees in the lowland areas are shallow rooted and the combination of heavy snow and wind will topple them.

When I first purchased Hawk's Nest there was a living eighty foot elm at the area where I planned to build the cabin. Its diameter was thirty inches which was measured four feet above ground level.

It was slightly over a year before I started to build the cabin. By that time the big elm was dead. Jerry came over with his chain saw and cut it up for firewood. He left the stump, which he carved, into a seat with a back on it. I still have a picture f his son Mike and daughter Katie sitting in the seat. They were two and four years old at the time.

There are still more than a hundred elms on the property. They grow from forty to sixty feet high before the bark beetle finds them and infects them with the fungus, which causes Dutch Elm Disease. Matt and I measured one living elm that had a height of seventy-two feet. Its trunk diameter was only seven inches.

The surviving elms produce seeds when they are still young compared to mature trees of other species such as oak .. An elm three inches in diameter may begin producing seed. Perhaps one of them will produce an offspring that is immune to the fungus or resistant to the advance of the bark beetle.

This morning I took my Brunton Compass and measured one hundred feet from another elm tree and took an angle reading on its height. The angle was thirty-five degrees, which makes the tree seventy feet tall. We now have two very tall living elm trees near the house.

Here is data on trees that are known to be twenty-five years old. The age is known since I transferred them as seedlings from the woodland and brush areas twenty-three years ago. (all numbers are rounded. The first number is diameter in inches and the second is height in feet).

Poplar 12-72, Red Maple #1 14-47, Red Maple #2 12-58, White Pine 13-38, Commercial Moraine Locust 9-47, Juneberry 6-27, Hawthorn 7-28, Hemlock 13-51, Frog Pond Elm 11-71. The large Sugar Maple where I built the cabin is 38 inches in diameter and 98 feet tall

Red Maple # 1 was attacked by some disease about ten years before this measurement. The disease peeled off a strip of bark about six feet long and six inches wide. Red Maple # 2 grows on the edge of a small long depression that contains lush grass since it retains moisture.

Yesterday I cleared out some blue beech trees from around a white pine that I planted fifteen years ago. The pine is twenty-five feet tall and has scraggly lower limbs. Clearing the beech away will give it a chance at lateral development. I wanted to preserve the pine since pine and oaks are the two best animal habitat trees in this area. This pine is a survivor of seedlings that Jerry gave me. It will be interesting to see changes that take place in the tree now that I have cleared a twelve-foot circle around it. I dare not clear much more than this since I don't know the strength of the trunk, which was in its infancy and damaged by a buck rub. The buck rub scar is a long, five-inch wide portion without bark. I placed wire around the trunk to a height of four feet. This should be enough to discourage any more buck rubbing. There are trees that I have known for more than thirty years. They comfort me as I make my rounds. They are old and I feel a comradeship with them. It is easy to understand why many Asians worship at the base of old trees, which are the world's oldest living life forms. When we were in Taiwan we saw many altars constructed at the base of ancient trees.

THE TREES IN THE FOREST

The typical northern climax forest has hemlock, beech, and maple. Some other trees add to the mix. Usually these other trees are remnants from the pioneer trees that began to occupy farmland or drained wetlands. The following is a short discussion of the trees that dominate our forest.

Hemlock

When I wanted siding for the cabin I went to a local lumber dealer and asked the owner to cut hemlock boards an inch thick and trim them on both sides. When the boards were delivered they were quite heavy. I stacked them on a flat surface with one-inch wide pieces of wood between them. Once their residue of moisture evaporated they were light in weight.

The hemlock boards were given an extra month to dry before I used them. The dividing slats were shifted every couple of days. I calculated that this would avoid large-scale shrinkage once the boards were in place and the summer sun worked on them. Hemlock proved to be a good siding material. The top of each nailed board was lapped over with the bottom of the board above it. Hence the term "lap siding." However, dry boards split quicker than wet boards. Fortunately there was a minimum of splitting. Irene painted the lower boards a dark green and I painted the upper boards. The color blended in well with the setting.

The Eastern Hemlock *(Tsuga canadensis)* grows to a maximum of seventy feet with a two-foot diameter. There are many trees at Hawk's Nest that have reached and slightly exceeded this general maximum.

Our hemlock grows in two large clusters, one just below the Ridge Trail and the other at the western entrance to the forest. These are both moist areas. Some of the western entrance trees are in wet soil and some of them are blown over in high winds. The Ridge Trail trees are on sloping ground and seem pretty well established. We named this area "the cathedral" because the trees dampen any noise and they maintain a green canopy throughout the winter. It creates a peaceful spiritual atmosphere.

As the hemlock grows it keeps its dead lower limbs and the tree expands and grows over them. Most other trees shed their lower limbs as they die off. The hemlock has flat needles and produces small seed cones when mature. It is the state tree of Pennsylvania. The young hemlocks have smooth bark while the old hemlocks have bark divided into rectangular blocks. The young hemlock bark might be described as flaky.

There were several medium-sized hemlock trees blown down during one huge windstorm. An interesting phenomenon occurred. on many of these. Several upright limbs on the down trees shot up and became trunks of new trees that were supplied moisture from the roots that were still in contact with the ground.

Generally hemlock is not used in construction since it splits easily and it is not used for firewood either because of its creosote production.

Bruce Boland, an outdoors man, has been a friend of mine for many years. We have often shared many adventures together. When Bruce and I camped at Hawk's Nest and used hemlock in the campfire we were often showered with sparks. When we tried to cut up some of the large hemlock logs the knots created by the old limb joints refused to be axed. The ax would bounce off these and create a hazardous situation.

Bruce, a true outdoors man, has been a friend of mine for more than thirty years. We traveled to Europe together and have had many adventures in the outdoors. He is a wild food specialist. When I visit him on his ridge in West Virginia he often serves such items as poke salad, wild berries, wild roots and nuts as well as wild game. But I digress.

The main use of hemlock in days of yore was in the tanning industry. There is a road south of Lake Erie named Tannery Road as well as in many streets in the local villages with that name.

Most of the original local tannery roads have been renamed since tannery operations ceased in the region. However, the names still appear on old,maps of this area.

Young hemlock trees make a good hedge since they are easily trimmed and grow in a compact form. They shed their needles quickly when cut so they do not make a good Christmas Tree. The green needles contain vitamin C and makes an acceptable tea. It was one of the teas used to prevent scurvy in pioneer days.

Both old and young hemlocks are trees of beauty. They are appreciated for their cover in winter as well as for their provision of food for wildlife. Their small cones are especially attractive to squirrels.

Beech

The American Beech *(Fagus granifolia)* are about the same girth and height as the hemlocks when they are full grown, that is, seventy feet high and three feet in diameter. They take a little longer to get there though. The majority of our beech trees grow above the Ridge Trail where the land is well drained. Here is found the typical beech-birch-maple forest with the birch being the yellow birch.

Of all our trees, the beech provides the best firewood. It splits easily and does not shed bark. In short, they are a clean firewood.

Beechnuts litter our forest floor every autumn. I have not noticed any good years and bad years. These nuts feed a variety of wildlife including grouse, squirrels, chipmunks, raccoons, wood ducks, turkey, grosbeak, blue jay, nuthatch, titmouse, bear, porcupine, fox, grackle and mice. Beech trees are the breadbaskets of our forest.

The beech has a beautiful smooth light gray bark, which would be an ideal place to carve one's initials. We would not like that to be done to our trees.

One of the problems in forest management concerning beech is their habit of sending up new shoots from their roots and from their abundant seeds. There are several areas in the woods where a cluster of six to ten-foot high beech trees compete with each other. In autumn these clusters are like areas of gold as their pale yellow leaves shimmer in the sunlight. Unfortunately the beech is one of the forest saplings that encroach on my trails and cutting them out is a chore that I regret.

When an opening occurs in a beech grove the trees next to the opening will send a limb into the opening and it quickly enlarges in diameter. This extending limb will usually get out of balance and will be broken when wet snow gathers on it. These broken limbs would supply me with enough firewood in any winter if I took the time to gather them.

Maple

Sugar and red maple grow in the forest but it is the red which sends its many winged seeds to the clear areas of the land to form a new colony. The sugar maple probably sends out as many seeds but these are readily eaten by a host of critters.

The maples grow in all areas of Hawk's Nest, but are mature in the forest. There are several isolated trees of both species in and about the brush areas and transplanted near the house. The forest maples are about sixty feet high and nearly two feet in diameter. A red maple I planted near the house
twenty five years ago is fifty-eight feet high and twelve inches in diameter.

The big sugar maple *(Acer saccharum)* at the cabin site is ninety-eight feet high and three feet, two inches in diameter. Another sugar maple is found two hundred feet to the south. This twin is a wolf tree which is a tree that grows by incorporating several trunks. This happens when a small tree is cut off or girdled by rabbits. This will cause it to send up several shoots, which if left alone will grow into each other as they mature. Our twin tree had at least five trunks grown together. Ron Boone, another naturalist friend of mine, said that multiple trunks was an indication of a wetland habitat.

When deer chew off the main tip of a small tree, the tree will respond by growing two new leader tips. This hinders development of the tree as the two new trunks compete for dominance. If this occurs in a prize tree then one of the new tips must be pruned.

The south twin maple was about seventy feet high when it began to die off. This tree would have a section of bright red leaves long before the other trees started changing leaf colors. The other big maple is always a brilliant orange in autumn. The trunks of the south twin started dying at the rate of one each year. Windstorms usually brought them down. Jim cut up two of them for his firewood.
The third trunk hung up there for about two years before it fell. When I cut it up there were many tunnels in the wood filled with fat white larva about two inches long. I photographed these for posterity. They were probably the larvae of the horntail fly. These larvae are usually host to the parasitic larva of the ichneumon fly.

The fourth trunk broke off at about twenty feet. It still has a connection with the ground and sends out a branch with leaves on it every year. The fifth trunk, which was in the center never fell, but its top broke off at about twenty feet. It is riddled with pileated woodpecker holes and we often see that bird running up and down the dead trunk in winter. We also see cardinals, blue jays, crows, white-breasted nuthatch, red-bellied woodpeckers, hairy woodpeckers, downy woodpeckers, chickadees, juncos, and titmouse on it in winter. In summer the dead trunk is a favorite resting-place for flickers. It is often a thrilling sight to look out from our dining room window and see a hawk perching at its very top.

The red maple (Acer rubrum) is identified by its three lobed leaves. Its seed germinates quickly and for that reason it is found in every land habitat of Hawk's Nest. Like many forest trees, the red maple has light colored smooth bark when young and shaggy dark colored bark when old. It is typically a swamp tree and woodcutters refer to it as "swamp maple." It flourishes at the perimeter of the swamp as well as in all other wetland areas that I do not cut over. The sugar maple is more successful in the upland than the red.

The red maple is considered a "soft" maple while the sugar maple is referred to as a "hard" maple. What I have observed is the red maple grows faster and decays faster than the sugar maple. The red maple does not make as reliable furniture, tool handles, or fence posts compared to the sugar maple. Sugar maple is superior to red maple for heating. Their differences are apparent in a campfire. In order to observe this you have to identify the species before you build the fire.

When I was a youngster our gang, which was led by my older brother, used to have a sugar maple trail. We would dig and cut off a small root and put a soda bottle on it. When we took our walks in the woods **we** had a refreshing cool drink of maple sap. I never did quite understand how the roots provided the sap.

The maple syrup industry is strong in our area and we are often asked by syrup producers if we would like our trees tapped. They would give us maple syrup in return. We don't do that, but we do buy syrup from local producers. On any early March morning one can see the tapped trees and plastic hose lines leading to the collecting tanks. Fresh local maple syrup is one of the perks of living in this region.

The winged maple seeds are eaten by a variety of wildlife including many birds. Apparently they prefer the sugar to the red since sugar maple seedlings are rare compared to the red. There is a difference in the smell of the crushed seeds of the two species. Perhaps there is a difference in the taste of the seeds to the animals. Deer, porcupine, and rabbits eat maple bark and twigs. Beaver will cut down maples, but they obviously prefer poplar if they can get it.

Black Cherry (Prunus serotina)

Our most commercially valuable forest tree is the wild black cherry. I have used the term "wild" in front of the name since youth when we used to climb them to their very height of sixty feet or more. We hollowed out an elderberry shoot as a pea shooter to propel the green cherries at each other. We ate the ripe cherries by the handful. I still do this

I do not know anyone who is as pleased with the taste of the wild cherry as I am. Most people I offer them to take a few cherries, try them, and refuse any more. The juice has an astringent quality to it.

Our wild cherry trees are many and they dominate the southeast comer of the properly. These range in size from mature trees thirty inches in diameter and seventy feet in height. Local sawmills have made us offers on the cherry but we do not wish to sell them at this time. Their wood is in demand in the veneer industry.

Our trees provide abundant fruit, which are consumed by all mammals, many birds and me. Once the fruit ripens I cannot resist their acrid flavor. In the past I have made wine and jelly from the fruit. Today, I am content to eat many handfuls during their season and spit the large round seeds into an area where I would like a new tree to grow.

The black cherry has a unique bark that splits into rectangular and square patterns. This exposes the red inner bark. Young trees have smooth bark with distinct horizontal lines.

The black cherry makes an excellent firewood. It is easily split. As one friend put it, "the logs split as if hit by a judo chop."

The wild black cherry tree creates our most abundant snags. These are dead trees that make a home for wildlife. Many are hollow. However, many of our live trees are also hollow with a living bark and wood growing around the hollow area .. These trees are usually around twenty inches, or more, in diameter and for some reason, unknown to me, develop a hollow center. Others just have openings somewhere along the trunk of the tree.

Yellow Birch

When I first saw the yellow birch many years ago I must have spent an hour looking at its twigs and leaves. To this day I still think its twigs and leaves are the most attractive of all trees. They are like an oriental painting, delicate but strong in color.

The yellow birch *(Betula lutea)* can be found scattered throughout our forest. When I constructed the first walking trail into the woods I purposely ran it near two large yellow birch. I have assisted these two trees by cutting away the competing vegetation around them. Both of these trees are about fifteen inches in diameter and thirty feet high. There are much larger yellow birch in the deeper parts of the forest.

The yellow birch is identified by its bronze bark, which peels in papery curls. In older trees the bark peels in coarse scaly plates. The curls make good fire starters, even in wet weather.

This is the birch of commercial importance. We are prone to think of white birch when birch is mentioned, but most, probably eighty percent of products with the label of birch are made from yellow birch.

Birch seeds are important as a late winter food for wildlife. Birch seeds can be seen on the top of crusted snow after a brisk wind. The seeds are very small and are housed in a small protective sheath cone. Usually the seeds are shaken loose before the cone falls.

Yellow birch wood is heavy and is good firewood. The birch tree is short-lived compared to most other species. A three hundred year-old yellow birch tree would be a museum piece.

Hornbeam

Our hornbeam *(Ostrya virginiana)* are on their way out of the forest even though they may last another hundred years. Somehow, the beech and maple do them in. The black cherry is also making inroads into the hornbeam territory.

The hop hornbeam tree, as it is sometimes called, is identified by its vertical peely bark that comes off in thin strips. It is mentioned here because of its large numbers along the eastern line overlooking the abandoned railroad bed.

The name hop hornbeam is the result of its clusters of leafy, hop like bladders, each with a small, nutlike seed attached inside at its base. To some the staminate catkins also resemble hops.

Some references list this tree as ironwood, which is a term often used to identify the blue beech *(Carpinus caroliniana)* which I first knew as the muscle tree due to its sinewy growth habit. Our blue beech trees grow on the creek floodplain as well as on the edges of the forest. Both trees have tough wood that can be used for firewood.

George Petrides in his *Field Guide to Trees and Shrubs* lists *Carpinus* as Ironwood and *Ostrya* as hornbeam, a name given to the tree because it was used to yoke oxen together. At least that is the legend.

The fruits of both trees are eaten by a variety of birds. Wood from these trees decay rapidly on the forest floor. A pile made of blue beech practically disappears within two years. I have stacked blue beech limbs and small trees in one particular spot for twenty years and one would have to be a scientist to determine that brush piles were made in that area.

The small hornbeam grove at the eastern line is an interesting area to observe. The light here seems different than in the other woodland sections. The blue beech or muscle tree is more of a nuisance than a pleasure, but its sinewy trunk is an interesting addition to the study of trees. I did use, at one time, the small trunk of a blue beech as a lever to dislodge my stuck tractor from some ruts. It proved to be a strong wood.

Each section of our forest has a different feel and smell to it. The different odor is obvious on damp days. Sometimes I feel a mood change as I move from the cluster of hemlocks to the beech and then to the hornbeam. My senses seem activated to these changes as I walk from one area to another. Wet days are days of low barometric pressure and the air is liberated from the ground bringing with it the aroma of the soil and the decayed leaves of trees.

Porcupine *(Ereythizon dorsatum)*

When I first strolled in the deep woods in winter I noticed lots of hemlock twigs on the snow and I assumed it was some natural process since I grew up in a deciduous forest where branches and leaves were always on the ground. I had no experience with native hemlock. It was much later when I noticed a porcupine in the limbs of a medium sized hemlock tree and made the connection with the twigs and little limbs on the ground.

When we first moved to Hawk's Nest Everett would report seeing a porcupine on his walks with Lobo. The dog was under his command and so there were no confrontations. It would be several years before I would see a porcupine in our woods.

After Lobo died we acquired a male puppy, an Australian Shepherd (Bear dog) mixed with something else. The dog roamed the woods freely and one snowy day I noticed that he was carrying a scrubbing brush in his mouth. It wasn't a brush but a mouthful of porcupine quills. We rushed Bear to the veterinarian who kept him overnight and removed the quills. The vet said he didn't feed or water overnight dogs.

As soon as I brought Bear home he rushed around the barn scooping up mouthfuls of snow. When I filled his water bowl he emptied it completely and continued scooping up snow. Finally, he had enough.

About two months later with snow still on the ground, Bear came back with ten new quills in his face. The vet counted them. I was going to pull them out myself but daughter April rushed the dog to the vet before I could get to it. Another stay for Bear dog and sixty dollars more went to the vet. This scene was repeated again a year later. Bear dog was a slow learner.

Despite Bear's problems we are fortunate to have porcupines in our woods since they are somewhat rare in Pennsylvania. They have a narrow range in the western part of the state extending from the New York border into West Virginia.

Hemlock is their preferred tree and once I learned to recognize their gnawing I found that they will gnaw on maple, birch, beech, and the arrow-wood viburnum. I believe they also chewed some of the boards on the bridge and one morning after a light snow their tracks appeared around the salt block. In deep snow they will stay in a single tree, sometimes for many months in the same tree as they pile up the cuttings below it.

The porcupine moves slowly and the one I saw moved at a snail pace as it climbed higher in the hemlock tree. It looked to be about twenty pounds, as it was the size of our dog Lobo who weighed twenty pounds. The porcupine here was about the size of one I came upon while hiking in Kluane National Park in western Canada. This one left its resting-place and walked across the rim of a six-foot waterfall right in front of me.

The Canadian porcupine was gray black while the one in our woods was black with white tips of its quills plainly visible. Both porcupines I saw made no sound although I have been told that they squeal, bark, chatter, whine, moan, mew, grunt, and cough.

Literature from the Game Commission states that they are subject to mange and autopsies have verified a large number of parasites on them. It is hard to imagine where a secretive animal such as the porcupine would pick up so many parasites..

Of course porcupines do not shoot out their quills which are very loose and may be shed if the animal turns quickly. According to the experts previously mentioned, bobcats and mink have been known to kill porcupines without harm to themselves. We have mink dens in our woods and we have seen bobcats passing through Hawk's Nest. Thus our resident porcupines have to be cautious.

THE POND

When Hawk's Nest was first purchased we planned on building a shelter by the creek. In order to get to the creek from Elgin Road we had to traverse a wet area about an acre in size? A narrow dry roadway led through the wet area and we made regular forages to the creek over that dry area.

Since there were no structures on the property I drove my pick-up truck to the edge of this wet area, parked the truck on a level surface and set up a campfire. There was a cap on the back of the truck and a sleeping mattress on the floor of the bed. Jerry and his neighbor Daley each had a horse grazing on the land. Jerry also had a large bull and Daley a cow. They kept the wet area cut over to provide forage for their animals They had also cleared other large patches of land.

One weekend, when I was camping, a thunderstorm came up. This confined me to the truck but it was almost dark so I decided to go to sleep. As lightning flashed around I felt the truck rising from the ground. It was Jerry's big red bull rubbing against the back of the truck. This jostling occurred throughout the night.

Bruce agreed to bring up a load of locust posts from the property we had in Fayette County, Pennsylvania since he had a long bed pickup truck and mine was only six feet. Bruce picked up the locust poles I had previously cut and delivered them to Hawk's Nest. It was August and the ground he had to cross looked to be dry enough for a crossing.

The truck with the extra weight of twelve long locust poles sunk in the ground up to the front axle. When Bruce tried to back out the truck also sank up to the rear axles. We unloaded the poles and tried jacking the rear up but the jack worked its way into the mud though it was on a rock that we had placed under it.

Our dilemma was observed by Daley as he brought grain to his horse and cow. He went home and returned with a battery operated winch that he attached to the back of the truck and the other end to his car. Instead of pulling the truck out of the mud it pulled the car toward the truck.

In a short time Jerry was on the scene. He noticed that Bruce had a power winch on the front of his truck. He asked if it worked and Bruce assured him that it did. Jerry walked the hook and cable about twenty feet away and attached it to a good-sized maple tree.. Bruce turned on the winch and it extracted his truck. However, he was now on the wrong side of the muck.

After much ado we found railroad ties up at the entrance and made a bridge to retrieve the truck. We carried the locust poles to the creek. I later filled the ruts made by the truck with rocks and other debris.

On the next weekend visit I started building the shelter with the poles. I had four poles in the ground and their tops tied together with wire since driving nails into dry locust wood was almost impossible. Building this shelter did not seem to be the good idea I once thought it was and I abandoned the project and piled the poles along the fence line. Eventually I used them for the first pier on the pond. The locust wood held up very well for this purpose.

The wet grassy area was a hindrance to getting to the creek by vehicle. The large flat area by the creek was an ideal camping spot, but not easily accessible. The wet area was not classic wet land, yet it was not dry enough to use. The decision was to construct a pond in this wet area.

Farmer Al took me to visit his Amish friend who had a pan. A pan in this case is a wheelbarrow type structure. The driver held the pan while his horse pulled it forward. The pan held about a yard of dirt. When the horse got to the end of the dig area the driver would tilt the pan and empty it then return for another load.

The Amish fellow said it was too much of a challenge for the size of pond I wanted and suggested we "get a dozer." Al said he would think about it and advise me.

While waiting for the advice Bruce and I went to a fellow on Route 6 that had a sign advertising construction work. We talked to the man for about a half-hour. He couldn't understand where the property was located even though it was seven miles from his place. Bruce pulled out his topographic map of the area. The man could not read a map so we made our exit.

Al recommended we go to the other side of Union City and talk to the Shreve Brothers. They had two dozers as well as other heavy building equipment. They agreed to do it.

The brothers brought their smaller dozer to the property and began pushing topsoil to one side. The dozer sank in the mud and couldn't move. The second dozer was brought to pull out the first. It too sank in the mud. It took a full day to get both dozers free by using cables and a big truck. One Shreve brother said the area was too wet to build a pond. What? Let's hear that again.

.   While dealing with the Shreves I made a discovery about one of their hobbies. Their farm was in the dairy business but one of the brothers was also into raising oddities, which included ornamental shrubs and fruit trees. He had six American Chestnut trees, which he procured from a company in Michigan. There was a small forest in Michigan that had chestnut trees which escaped the blight. The Shreve trees were about ten feet high. I made it a point to check on the trees every once in a while. When the brothers both died about five years later the stock of trees was sold and I was not able to find out what happened to them after that.

Once while walking through the woodland of Warren County I found two American Chestnut trees that were growing from two different old stumps. The trees were about fifteen feet high. Both of these trees perished within three years of my discovery of them. I am certain there are chestnut trees growing from old stumps all over the Pennsylvania forest lands. Perhaps some of them will survive to reproduce.

My plan for a pond was not abandoned. I decided to dig a diversion ditch at the upper end of the slope and cut off the surface water supply to the flat area. The vegetation on the wet area was mostly grass on which the animals grazed. It was not typical wetland. The ground material under the grass was clay and silt deposited by glaciers fourteen thousand years ago. This material was reworked by the creek in its periodic flooding.

A year passed and it was July once again. Jerry and Daley had removed their livestock. Jerry presented me with two big steaks from Big Red. These were a real treat.

My first step that summer was to contact contractor Tomcho and Sons. They agreed to try excavating the wet area that was considerably drier now. When Joe appeared with a big bucket front loader I told him the weatherman predicated rain. He said if he listened to the weatherman he would never get any work done.

Joe's son Steve came a little later with a small dozer on flat bed truck. I showed them the north property line where the remnants of a barbed wire fence hung loosely on rotting posts. They immediately got to work.

Three weeks later they had a one and half acre excavation with the deepest hole at nine feet. They made a road around the excavation with the material excavated. I paid them and they removed their equipment. Joe said it would take at least two years for the pond to fill since the area was fed by underground springs and a small trickle from an above ground stream which Farmer Al called a "spring run,"

There was a sticky blue clay layer ten inches below the surface of the grass area on the pond flats. This was probably contributing to the sinking of vehicles. Once the Tomcho's got through this clay area the digging was dry and easy. I dug down to this blue clay area on the fringes of the excavation and enlarged the pond by another six hundred square feet. I must have moved three hundred wheelbarrow loads, which I used to fill in the low spots of the road. We all enjoyed making statues and cups out of the blue clay. Al's grandchildren took home a basket of the material. They returned a few days later to show us their creations. I made a statue of a llama and baked it in one of my campfires then later painted it. The creation was supposed to be a giraffe but it turned out to be a llama.

There was a downpour of rain in September and the pond, which was to take two years to fill, was up to the brim from the five inches of rain that fell in twenty four hours. It was testimony to the drainage pattern that kept the land wet.

A month later I hired Joe's son Martin who had a big backhoe and front loader. He dug out more of the pond and touched up some rough bank areas. I paid him five hundred dollars, making the total cost of the pond five thousand dollars.

We began to transfer minnows from the creek to the pond. Everett set out his minnow traps each evening and every morning emptied the minnows into the pond. He probably transferred fifteen hundred of them before he ceased that activity.

Everett would also transfer the trout he caught in Lilley Run to the pond. His count was thirty-one trout. Everett also made a deal with Jerry's teen-age son Mark. He would pay Mark fifty cents an inch for every trout he brought to the pond. Mark earned about seventy-five dollars in the summer he worked at that task.

One evening Jerry showed up with five yellow perch about six inches long. I protested putting them in the pond fearing they would discourage the trout. After listening to his arguments I agreed to let the perch in. It turned out to be a good move since the perch prospered and the trout didn't. I reasoned that there was no gravel bed with running water over it for the trout to spawn. The perch grew to twelve inches by the following year. Soon there was an abundance of perch in all sizes. I would catch six for a meal and have three meals every summer for the next eight years.

Catfish came into the pond from out of nowhere. Perhaps they were among the transferred minnows but we never noticed them since we all went down to the pond for each minnow transfer. Rumor has it that catfish and carp are transported on the feet of migrating waterfowl. I don't know this to be true, but it is an explanation. However, catfish were now in the pond and we ate them also. When we fished for catfish we would use sinkers and worms. We sometimes would drag a snapping turtle back to shore. Fortunately, none were ever hooked deep enough to cause trouble. We eventually gave up fishing for catfish in the deep water..

We all, except Everett, swam in the pond. There were inner tubes and other floating devices. I built a ten-foot pier and the kids did cannonball jumps from it. We purchased a second-hand fiber glass boat and took evening rides in it. When we fished from the anchored boat the snapping turtles would come over and swim around the boat giving us a good view of them. We soon started taking bread to the pond and feeding the turtles with it.

Meanwhile other aquatic life moved in -Dragonflies, damselflies, water snakes, muskrats, bull frogs, leopard frogs, green frogs, giant water bugs, water boatman, water walking sticks, leeches and clams. The water walking stick is not a walking stick but an insect known as water measurer, a member of the water scorpions. They have a vicious bite.

A Great Blue Heron pair began nesting on Al's property and making regular visits to the pond. It started nesting the third year after the pond was finished and has built annual nests ever since. Usually they only produce one offspring.

The Canada Goose nested in the swamp and made the pond their recreation area. There was one pair the first four years, then there were two pairs, then three. There was a population of Canada Goose about ten years ago and an excess breeding population still remains to this day. There were once eight nesting pairs. This year, as I write this, there are three pairs that bring their goslings to the pond every day and retreat up the creek to Al's sanctuary each evening.

Bats began to patrol the dusky skies over the pond at sunset. They are still at it. They swoop over our heads as we take our evening walks. We count as many as six but they flit overhead so fast it is difficult to get an exact count when their numbers increase in the sky just after sunset. The number must be around a dozen.

The vegetation around the pond changed over the years.. After more than twenty years of pond the shrub vegetation now includes the obnoxious willow, bush honeysuckle, red-osier dogwood, and arrow-wood viburnum, I keep these reduced in size by cutting them at their base every two to three years. There are also the non-shrubby plants of narrow leaf and broadleaf cattail, nut grass, sedges, blue iris, swamp milkweed, common milkweed, dogbane, poison hemlock, buttercup, ironweed, boneset, goldenrod, redroot cyprus, and bulrush.

Barn swallows and tree swallows skip over the pond all summer. The kingfisher sits briefly in the big maple at the lower edge of the pond and frantically dives in and out. Bitterns, green herons, and ospreys visit us. The green heron nested on the property one season.

Migratory waterfowl which pass through and stop, mostly in spring, include common merganser, red breasted merganser, bufflehead, hooded merganser, greater and lesser scaups, blue teal, green teal, eared grebe, horned grebe, piedbilled grebe, wood duck, mallards, common tern, sandpipers, coot, greater yellow legs, redhead (twice), shoveler, golden eye, and baldpate.

One late afternoon as we sat in the dining room a large bird appeared and hovered over the pond. A few seconds later it dove into the water. We knew it was an osprey since we have a print of an osprey on our dining room wall. We saw the blackish bands on its tail, its white crown, white throat and white underparts. It has visited us at least once each year since we first noticed it.

A whistling swan with a bloody rump showed up during waterfowl hunting season. We didn't go down to the pond while swan was there but watched it for about a week. One day, about noon, it took to the air, circled the pond four times and headed south. I was fortunate to have witnessed this event.

Perhaps we made an error

The Game Commission advertised a sale of largemouth bass . One hundred bass could be purchased for ninety-nine dollars. That was twelve years ago. I ordered a hundred with Everett's okay. We received a postcard telling us to pick up the bass at the commission building in the town of Starbrick, just outside of Warren.

Everett bought a thirty-gallon plastic trashcan and fitted a hose and bicycle pump to it. This was to aerate the water for the thirty-six mile drive from Starbrick. The night before the transfer he put twenty gallons of pond water in the trash can so the bass would be at home when they got there..

We drove to Starbrick along with April and her friend Laurel who were eight years old at the time. The girls practiced pumping air into the water.

We arrived at the designated place and I told the uniformed woman in charge that we had come to pick up the bass. We signed some papers and I gave her a check for the fish. She disappeared into a back room. When she emerged she was carrying a small six-cup sauce pan with water in it. The fish were in there and she assured us there were a hundred. They were little black dots swimming haphazardly in every direction. A deal is a deal. We dumped the pan into what seemed to be our huge reservoir and head home.

A fierce lightning storm came up and there was difficulty driving. The girls worked the pump although it seemed pointless considering the size of the fish and the twenty gallons of water. The storm was raging when we got to the pond. Lightning flashed and thunder rolled as Everett and I dumped the twenty gallons of water and pencil point fish into the pond. I figured they would be food for the perch. Everett agreed.

Two years later we were catching five-inch largemouth bass. Two more years and they were ten to twelve inches. We started eating those. We noticed a definite decrease in perch population..

We worried about the food situation for the bass. Matthew and I went to the Union City reservoir and caught thirty-seven blue gill, brought them back and dumped them in the pond. The pond ecology shifted from perch and minnows to bass and blue gill. The blue gill multiplied quickly. Today, many of them are the size of a large hand. When we take bread to feed the turtles the blue gill come to the site in schools.

Three years after the blue gill were introduced we invited some Amish friends to fish in the pond. About twelve of them showed up and had a bushel basket of fish when they left. We didn't know how to react to this and never invited them back.

Matthew enjoys fishing for the bass. The largest are about fifteen inches. One large one required weighing and it came in at slightly over four pounds. Matt insisted on putting that one back.

We still catch perch but they are not in the numbers of yesterday. Most perch catches are in the six to nine inch category. When we use the dip net to check on the minnows we seldom see perch in among them. Occasionally we will catch a fall fish around nine inches long or a large creek chub of similar length.

Snapping Turtles *(Chelydra serpentina)*

Even before we built the pond we had snapping turtles in the swamp and in the slow moving deep muddy bottom parts of the creek. The largest snappers are about the size of a nine inch paper plate. We find tiny snappers from time to time and we hustle these to the swamp where their protection is greater.

When we throw bread in for the fish, a large snapper comes and drives the fish away and takes the bread. We have named her Myrtle and we recognize her by a white scar on her head, She has been with us at least twenty-five years. We see her almost every year laying eggs in a hole drilled into clay. We also see other large females engaged in the same activity.

We often scan the pond with binoculars looking for waterfowl. The pond is slightly over a hundred and fifty feet from the house. A few years ago I noticed a lot of turbulence in the far corner of the pond. I went to check it out.

There were two huge snapping turtles rolling in the water which was flying in every direction. They ignored my presence on shore. It was either a fight over territory or some bizarre turtle mating ritual. Myrtle was not one of them.

They rolled and rolled and the water boiled around them. An hour passed and they were still rolling. I left them to their activity. A year later I witnessed the same commotion in one of the deeper pools of the swamp.

The snapping turtle can easily be identified by its round shell that is divided into blocks. It has a long tail with dinosaur bumps on it. The snapping turtle cannot retract its large head into the shell. The claws on its feet will easily scratch and tear your skin. It is a vicious predator of fish, frogs, salamanders, crayfish, other turtles, birds, mammals and carrion. It will also eat plants, and earthworms. We stopped fishing with sinkers, bobbers and worms after we caught several snappers.

Myrtle probably weighs twenty pounds judging from snappers that I have seen weighed. One snapper found and captured near Waterford, seventeen miles west of Hawk's Nest, weighed thirty-six pounds.

The female snapper lays anywhere from a dozen to six dozen eggs in a hole six inches deep. Usually the hole is drilled into a hill with good drainage. When I constructed a new small bridge where water run off enters the pond I made a clay ramp for the bridge. Three different turtles laid eggs in it the same month of May when I completed the bridge. The young turtles hatch anywhere from eight to eighteen weeks. If they hatch in late autumn the young will winter over in the nest.

When we first moved here, there was a snapping turtle nest with the eggs exposed. I reached in and took two of them to cabin and boiled them for ten minutes and ate them. They tasted like mud but were not unpleasant. I never repeated this ritual.

One can often see many snappers migrating in the spring by driving on our area roads. They are on the road and beside the road. When on the road we stop our vehicle and hurry them to the other side. Some large snappers resist this hurrying and so I take a flat shovel and scoop them up and deposit them a few feet from the road. If the snappers are small we put them in our vehicle and drive them to Hawk's Nest for release. One can't have too many snapping turtles.

The muskrat is another of our interesting water animals. They live in the pond, the swamp and work the creek. They make their home in the banks of the pond and on the small islands that I constructed in the swamp.

If the muskrat population were left unchecked they would destroy the pond with their tunnels. I spend a lot of time each spring filling in muskrat tunnels in the road around the pond.

The muskrat body is around twelve inches long with a vertical flat tail adding eleven more inches to its length. A better description of the tail would be to say it was laterally compressed. Its hind feet are partly webbed.

When we walk along the pond in summer we often come upon muskrats feeding in the white clover which grows abundantly on any mowed area. The muskrat also eats cattails and grasses. We often find clam shells after muskrats have dined upon the contents. Their droppings are on all the rocks, which I have placed along the edge of the pond.

Nine year old Matt with muskrat
Muskrat *(Ondatra zibethiclls)*

Most female muskrats produce four to seven young, but some heavy breeders may breed several times and produce forty offspring in a breeding year. Some females may have as many as six litters a year. Jim traps them each year and gets over a hundred from the pond, swamp, and stream.

The muskrat is the country's leading fur animal. The creation of artificial fibers and the campaign against trapping has diminished their value. A muskrat pelt brought three dollars twenty years ago. Today they bring a dollar each in a good selling year. Jim traps to keep the population in check and to enjoy a hobby he had throughout his life.

I have built ponds on every rural property I have ever owned. I had constructed a road across the dam of a pond I made on a small stream in Fayette County. I mentioned this previously as the source of locust poles. I had neglected this property for over a year when I drove across the dam. My pickup truck broke the surface and sank into the muskrat tunnels below. The truck had sunk up to its front axle a foot below ground level. I put the four-wheel drive into motion and then the back wheels broke into the hole below. I had to hire a wrecker to extract the truck.

Eventually the property was sold to Bruce and the last time I visited it the muskrats had completely broken the dam and running water eroded it down to the drainpipe four feet below.
Bruce no longer lives in that area and is keeping the property as an investment. He receives a small royalty from a gas company that drilled on an adjacent property. This pays the taxes.

Bruce lives a solitary life in a cabin without running water on two hundred acres of wild land in West Virginia. He works as a part-time instructor at three different colleges. His only visitors to his property are gas well tenders and seasonal deer hunters who supply him with venison.

We exchange letters at least once a week. His mailbox is a quarter-mile from his cabin. Thoreau would have found Bruce to be a kindred spirit as I do.

If I did not fill the muskrat holes and tunnels at Hawk's Nest the same situation would prevail. Filling muskrat tunnels is a never-ending chore..

There are muskrat signs in the winter pond. They come up for air when the ice is thin and their breathing holes are obvious. The ice has been thirteen inches thick in some years and about seven inches thick in an average year so the muskrat takes a chance if it tries to swim the length of the pond when it is frozen over. I have found two dead minks in two separate years after the ice had melted. They are the biggest predators on our muskrats. I have also found a drowned gray fox in the pond after the winter ice was gone.

It is a delight to watch a muskrat in the water. It dives, surfaces and waves its rudder of a tail. However, once it sees a change in the shoreline, like a human standing there, it will dive down. It races along under water creating a V-shaped surface wave.

Muskrats at Hawk's Nest are eaten by mink, great horned owl, fox and our dog Bear when he corners one on land. He has jumped into the water after them but has never been successful in capturing one in the water. He will dig for them in their holes and tunnels on the road surface. Of course they are not there and I have a larger hole to fill. When he does catch one he eats every bit of it.

The frog pond is an ideal place to see frogs, snakes, and birds. The rock in the pond is a summer resting place for water snakes and will inhabit that space for about a week before moving on.

Water Snake

The northern water snake *(Nerodia sipedom)* is one of the great animals of the Hawk's Nest pond and environs. There are many of varying sizes. They are in the swamp, the frog ponds, and especially the pond. The largest are four feet in length and two inches in diameter at the fattest point.

It was an exciting moment when I first saw a three-foot water snake swimming merrily along with a green frog in its mouth. However, their main food is fish. They will also eat salamanders, tadpoles, and crayfish.

There was a twelve-inch water snake in distress on a mud flat a few years ago. It was slowly regurgitating small minnows and had ejected four of them before it noticed me and retired to another location.

Our water snakes have a crosscheck pattern reminiscent of rattlesnakes but not as bright. Some are simply gray above and lighter below.

One summer two boys from the west ridge brought a small checkered black and white snake for me to identify. They were disappointed when I told them it was an immature water snake. They were hoping for a copperhead. They were also disappointed when I told them there are no poisonous snakes in our county.

Our water snakes can be seen sunning on rocks in summer, especially in the main frog pond where there is a large rock near the center of it. As winter approaches the water snakes are still evident while our other snake species have sought refuge. When daughter April was three years old we walked to the edge of the flats. It was November and there was a large apple tree there that still had apples on it. I lifted her up and she took an apple.

We stood on the banks of the stream that emptied into Lilley Run. I looked down and saw that April was standing on a four-foot water snake. It wasn't moving and it was stretched out rather than coiled. Naturally, I whisked April off of it. The snake lay as if dead and only moved a little when I touched it with a stick. It was still lethargic when I put a stick under it and lifted its center from the ground.

Generally, a water snake will strike out for no apparent provocation. Snake fanciers consider them to be among the most vicious of the snake kingdom. One spring when our cats were still permitted outside they had a large water snake cornered on the mowed area. I quickly hustled them back to the house.

Water snakes like all snakes, turtles, frogs, toads, and other reptiles and amphibians are cold blooded. Their blood temperature duplicates that of the air around them. They are solar powered and when the temperature rises their activity rises I am now a little like that myself.

Once spring appears and summer is on the way I mow around the pond. When I repeat mowing I stick to the parameters that were first set in spring. The reason for this is because frogs, snakes and rodents inhabit the edge of the area not mowed. In the early years when I widened the road mowed area I more often than not decapitated some critters. One such unlucky creature was a beautiful three-foot long water snake. That bothers me to this day.

When a water snake finds a rewarding spot it will usually forage there for days. One such snake nestled on the left side of the pier all summer. When visitors came we could take them to the pier and let them see a water snake. When we mentioned the snake to one couple the woman went to their car and stayed there until her husband had finished his visit.

Dragonflies, Damselflies, and Others

Dragonflies and damselflies are everywhere but they are most abundant around the pond. These feed on small insects, which they capture on the wing. A dragonfly bite is painful but the chances of getting bitten by one is almost nil. Still they should be handled with care. Dragonflies rest with their wings open while damselflies rest with their wings closed over their backs.

Both insects lay eggs on water plants or in the water itself. The young nymphs develop where the eggs are laid. The nymphs go through several growing stages and eventually there is a final skin split and an adult emerges.

The dragonfly may travel several miles since it is a strong flyer. They are important in keeping mosquitoes and various flies under control. Dragonflies often travel in tandem, that is, one fly on top of another.

Sometime in mid-summer we walk to the pond and the air is full of light colored flying objects. These are the mayflies that live but a day in the air and then perish. Mayflies are unique in that they still molt after their wings have become functional. The adults do not feed. They seem to gather in swarms for one last hurrah.

Eggs of the mayfly are attached to stones and like most water flying insects the nymph goes through several stages before it becomes an adult. Sometimes the number of dead mayflies is so great they are washed up on shore before the fish can get at them. Let us hope they enjoy the nymph stage and apply the Tao proverb, "The journey is more important than the destination."

There are several species of mayflies at Hawk/s Nest and we identify them by size. We also have the Dobson fly which looks ferocious with the male pincers but is harmless. The pincers are used in mating. The eggs are laid on vegetation and the emerging larvae drop into water and spend three years growing up. We know the larvae as the hellgrammite, which is about two inches long. It would not win any prizes for beauty but fish love them.

Bullfrogs

Although the bullfrogs are in the swamp and creek they are best seen in the pond. They stake out territory in spring and can be heard making their deep hoarse "more rum" call throughout the breeding season. They always live near deep water.

The bullfrog (Rana catesbeiana) is eight inches long and dark green to black in color. Their tympanum, or eardrum, is as large as their eyes.

It is surprising to learn that the bullfrog will eat fish, smaller frogs, snakes, baby turtles, mice and any bird it can swallow. We tend to think of frogs as flying insect eaters. It will even eat its own young.

Tadpoles of the bullfrog take two years to mature. It is easy to mistake them for fish before they develop legs. They are fat and swim like fish. I once found a large water bug attached to a first year tadpole. The water bug never let go of the tadpole even after I scooped it into a small dish to examine it more closely. I eventually put them both back into the water. I might even have a picture of this somewhere in my lost picture files. The event was at a time when I carried a camera with me on every walk.

We get a count on our mature bullfrogs by walking slowly around the edge of the pond. Generally we count eight to ten in a given summer. There are probably a dozen on the property in any summer. There is always a resident bullfrog at the deep part of the creek near the bridge.

Monarch butterfly on swamp milkweed.

Pond Memories

All ponds are temporary features of a landscape. Ponds and swamps are constantly being filled in with sediment. Their banks are eroded by overflowing water as well as destruction by animals such as muskrats and woodchucks.

A healthy pond has an oxygen-carbon dioxide cycle similar to those described under trees. These two gases are passed back and forth between plants and animals in ponds just as they are in any other environment. Disruption in the cycle causes a disruption in the biotic life depending on that cycle.

Water plants release oxygen during daylight in the process of photosynthesis. When night arrives the plants and animals living in water depend on the dissolved oxygen since production of oxygen ceases. Oxygen is also added to pond water by the action of the wind roughing up the surface. Not much is added in this manner but what is added is needed.

Carbon dioxide is added by the decay of organic matter and from respiration of plants. It is difficult to imagine plants breathing under water but they do, in their own manner. There is also an addition of carbon dioxide by ground water and from the atmosphere. It is used in photosynthesis and the green plants are the beginning of the food chain.

Carbon dioxide forms a weak acid which breaks down and combines with lime to form calcium carbonate the basis for limey shells in animals such as clams and snails.

Vital to pond health is the turnover of water, which takes place twice a year as summer and winter decline. In summer there is layering of water temperature. When we go for a swim the surface water is warm and when we stand up in a deep place our feet feel the layering and the colder water below. This affects the comfort level of aquatic life.

There are four distinct habitats in a pond. These are the surface film or tension on the water, the open water, the basin or bottom and the shoreline. Even these habitats are broken into smaller units by limnologists, that is, the people who study ponds.

The film surface has large walking and skating insects on it. Water striders, whirling beetles and spiders are easily seen. Just under this film surface are water scorpions, mosquito larva, and an assortment of other larva.

The open water has our familiar menagerie of fish and a huge assortment of floating microscopic animals and plants known as zooplankton and phytoplankton. More will be said on this later.

The basin or bottom has the rooted plants and the insect larva that cling to them. There are snails, crayfish, clams, worms, larvae and bacteria. Bacterial action returns the decayed material at the bottom back into the system.

The shore has a variety of plants and animals living between land and water. An interesting plant study revealed some plants that were pollinated above water developed seeds that germinated and grew into new plants under water.

What we see around the pond are the large forms of plant and animal life. However, these large entities depend on the microscopic plants and animals, which form the basis of the web of life. One summer I borrowed a microscope and took water samples from the pond and swamp and studied them by placing drops of the water on glass plates. It was a jungle of unbelievable proportions.

Some of the animals and plants could be seen with the unaided eye but under the microscope they were dazzling. There were rotifers, flagellates, stentors, diatoms, flatworms, water fleas, hydra and a plethora of other creatures faintly remembered and I misplaced my notes so I mention those that come to mind. Also seen were amoebas and paramecium. What was also fascinating was the magnification of mosquito and many other larvae. Their movements were those in the dance of life. These creatures were living in a few drops of water. How many drops of water are in an acre of pond three feet deep. The microscopic life in the pond is in numbers unimaginable to the human mind.

The pond has many forms of plants under the water surface. In spring and autumn a few sections of pond surface has a slimy looking green mass floating upon it. These are green and blue-green algae, which can occur as single cells, flattened floating colonies or as filaments. These form masses in the spring of the year, then seem to disappear in the heat of summer, only to return in autumn. Trying to gather this surface algae on a stick does not work as the stick cuts through the soupy mass. The deeper algae will cling to the stick since it is of the filament type.

Watermilfoil *(Myriophyllum species)* is a common plant at the pond and the frog ponds while pondweeds dominate the swamp. There are several different species of milfoil and it is difficult to tell them apart.

The dominant plant form of the pond is coontail or hornwort. *(Ceratophyllum demersum)*. These appear as a carpet on the pond bottom. Gliding over them in a boat gives the appearance of a small forest under the water.

Once the coontail started forming they carpeted the pond bottom. This made swimming inconvenient and we no longer swim in the pond because of this as well as the increased beaver activity. Sometime in the last couple of years we began to consider the diseases spread by beavers.

In the past I have cleared several feet of the carpet from around the pier but it grew back quickly. If we wish to cool off by bathing in summer we go to the swimming hole in the creek.

As I walk along the shore with my walking stick I will put it into the water and pick up about a pound of the green carpet and toss it onto the shore where it will turn brown in a couple of days. This helps to keep the shallow shore area visible for observation of aquatic life and the large bass that swim along the shore..

Several times in the past, herbicide salesmen have stopped and given me a sales pitch on eliminating pond vegetation. They guarantee that it will not harm fish or other aquatic animal life. Since animal life depends on a base of vegetation I do not believe that statement to be true. Also if there were no vegetation we would have to start feeding the fish.

One autumn I started loading the boat with the carpet plants, wheeled them to the garden and covered my garden with them. I moved about twenty wheelbarrow loads from the pond to the garden. When spring arrived I spaded it under. There was no noticeable extra fertility in the garden that summer or the following summer. My small garden is fenced in since deer, raccoons, rabbits and woodchucks abound. On many mornings, I have found a rabbit or a woodchuck trapped in the garden fencing. One rabbit was observed eating the carpet vegetation.

What I call the carpet plants, milfoil and coontail, appear erect in the water when we pass over them in the boat. When they are brought to shore they collapse into a wet mass. In order to identify and study them the plants are put in a basin of clear water and separated. They can also be examined effectively after they have dried a couple of days. The dry plant mass is easily separated.

The herbicide salesmen refer to the water vegetation as weeds, which typically means a plant that is out of place. Our plants are out of place only when they interfere with our swimming or fishing. These plants provide food for ducks, muskrats, fish, insects and especially geese. The plants give fish a place of moderating temperature and the plants also produce oxygen. The plants are also home to bacteria and protozoa, which are supporting the web of pond life.

Generally algae is an indication of organic pollution. On of the ponds I constructed, at another location, the algae was so massive it looked like one could walk across the pond on it. This pond was in a confined basin that had run-off from a cattle grazing area. Runoff collecting ditches around this pond did not alleviate the situation.

The present pond has a twelve-inch diameter metal pipe which keeps the water from overflowing the pond banks except during very heavy precipitation and accumulated snow melting. There are also two six-inch pipes that are slightly above the level of the larger pipe. Beaver are constantly blocking all three pipes and it is a never ending chore to keep these water exits open.

There was a large amount of beaver debris on shore near the larger pipe. This was an accumulation from cleaning the entrance to the pipe. The debris consisted of milfoil, coontail, mud, rocks, and grass. When I finally went to wheelbarrow the debris to another location after six months there was a plethora of dog stinkhorn fungi *(Mulinus caninus)* growing on the pile. Their brilliant red tips and white sheaths were attractive against the brown debris. How did they get there?

THE FROG PONDS

There was a wet spot in the yard about sixty feet north of the house. Mowing was difficult and the lawn tractor was often hung up on the wet surface and had to be assisted to drier ground. The only solution was to create a running spring.

Everett and I started digging. Our plan was to get down to the layer that was forcing the water to the surface, create a wall and insert a pipe into it. We would landscape the area with the removed soil.

As we were digging we discussed the glacial activity in the area and how the ground was not disturbed for a few thousand years. The discussion continued in this manner until we found a pair of deteriorated leather boots. Everett said he would keep digging until he found a wallet.

Further digging revealed some flat stones set in the form of the letter A. Some farmer of yore had devised his own method of drainage. His lean-to type structures were clogged with mud and that is probably why the water came out at the surface. These stones set in the formation continued toward a small drainage depression thirty or more feet away. We didn't dig them all out. We did get a nice collection of flat stones, which are not plentiful in a glaciated area.

We set a plastic pipe in the newly created three-foot wall, which we had reamed out to a length of three feet. We had perforated the end of the pipe for two feet. Water began to flow freely from the pipe and we sealed the wall with clay to force any leaking water back into the perforations. Our Amish visitors drank freely of it. I was concerned because the area had cattle grazing on it for about thirty years, although the cattle had not been on it for three years. Eventually, I drank the water and washed my face and neck in it during the hot summer working days.

Once the house was built and a water system established there was no need for the spring so I built a small dam over the exit and created a sixteen-foot long pond that was two feet deep at its center. A basketball-sized boulder was placed on a mound just off the center of it. Daughter April and her friends waded in it just after its construction. It ceased to be a wading pool once vegetation started moving in.

Soon frogs moved in, followed by salamanders. The usual willow began to grow at the upper end and an autumn olive bush was transplanted beside it. Cattails moved into the upper end in the third year. A Great Blue Heron was standing in it one morning at sunrise. In the fourth year a red-winged blackbird built a nest in the cattails and a chipping sparrow built in the willow. People look for the first robin in spring but we look for the Red-winged blackbird. Robins are often seen in our deep woods in winter but the blackbird is here only in spring and summer

There was room for a second frog pond and it was constructed below the first. A plastic pipe was installed to direct water from the first frog pond. However there was a lot of seepage through the bank of the dam of the first frog pond. The second frog pond ended up eight feet in diameter. In its first year there were hundreds of frog egg masses in the water which was only a foot deep. The hard clay pan under the surface made further digging difficult.

Two black currant bushes were moved from the swamp and planted beside the second frog pond bank. This was followed by the transfer of bristly gooseberry from the woods and nannyberry from the flats.

There was an attempt to transplant four elderberry stalks and it looked like they would prosper. However, I had stacked some discarded cattail plants near them and decided to burn them when they dried out. This was done and the heat from the fire killed the four elderberry shoots. I had forgotten where they were there and had stacked the brush too close to them.

Three- fourths of the first frog pond was shortly taken over by cattails. There was nothing to do but wade in and root them out. Their root systems were extensive and I moved five wheelbarrow loads of cattails to the burn pile in the area previously mentioned.

A small area of cattails was left for the blackbird to build a nest if it so wanted. Besides, the cattail is indicative of a clean water environment and adds beauty to it. However, their aggressive nature requires constant vigilance.

Bonnie got the idea that it would be nice to have minnows in the upper frog pond. Matthew caught some small blue gill at the pond in a dip net. He transferred them to the upper frog pond. It was probably a mistake since the blue gill multiplied rapidly and the frogs and salamanders decreased rapidly although they were still in evidence. The only frog egg masses that survive are those hidden in the vegetation. The fish made their way through the pipe and also became residents of the second frog pond.

There are frogs, salamanders, water snakes, toads and blue gill living in some sort of biotic relationship in the frog ponds. The resident Great Blue Heron pair, raccoon and the water snake regulate the fish population. Occasionally we find a snapping turtle around the frog ponds.

Watermilfoil and coontail moved into the upper frog pond about ten years ago. It looks like a green carpet below the water level. We wish to keep the frog pond bottoms as clear of this carpet vegetation as possible. When I take up some of the plants to expose the bottom, I usually take up some soil with it thus deepening the pond. I check the dredge for tadpoles and salamanders before I place them on a pile.

A large water snake inhabits the frog ponds and it has been seen every year for the last five. I am not certain about the longevity of water snakes but it looks like the same one. There are also a few smaller water snakes in the pond area and these smaller ones are often seen sunning on the large rock in the upper frog pond. I have also moved some large rocks to the edge of the lower frog pond. One of the rocks is two feet in diameter. It is granite and rounded in the typical manner of glacial tumbling and transport. It was too heavy to pick up. I cut a piece of plywood two feet square and attached a chain to two places on it. Matthew and I levered the stone onto the platform and we pulled it up to the frog ponds with the lawn tractor, a distance of about a quarter mile.

Several blue water iris were transplanted from the creek to the lower frog pond as were marsh marigolds, daffodils, yellow water iris and some ferns. I also put in some small barberry bushes but inadvertently mowed them over when I mowed around the edges of the ponds.

Bonnie purchased two Koi fish in order to counteract the increase in watermilfoil and the algae that started to gather on the surface of the upper pond in early summer, She put one in each frog pond. The Koi is reputed to be a vegetation eater and has made some difference in the carpet if not the alga. The Koi is a carp a goldfish that is sterilized when imported into our country.

When spring peepers *(Hyla crucifer)* awaken in the swamp after a long winter nap they also wake up in the frog ponds. During the height of the peeping season they are serenading continuously. Sometimes, using caution, we can creep up on them and observe their throat expanding and contracting as they make their sales pitch.

The spring peeper is an inch and a half long and is classified as a tree frog. Its main identifying mark is an X on its green gray-brown back. It is mainly recognized by its shrill peeping which lasts a half-second in a series. We open our bedroom windows and the peepers sing us to sleep.

One summer evening as we returned from dining out we heard a "brack" noise. It was loud and was intermittent, every two minutes. We could not identity it but believed it to be some bird species. We walked around looking for the noise maker but could not find it.

The following evening the "brack" occurred again. We commented on it but went back to our pursuits. Ten-year old Laurel was visiting at the time. She took a flashlight and went outside to find the noisemaker. About ten minutes later she called to us from the north deck area of the house. The culprit was behind a flowerpot. The culprit was a small gray brown frog with a dark triangle on its head and stripes on its back. It was a northern cricket frog *(Acris crepitans)*. It was probably on the deck looking for spiders, which is reputed to be its favorite food. Of course it will also eat insects. After discussion of the "brack" we decided the call was more like someone hitting stones together. It was like hearing a noise under water.

A mature cricket frog is about one and a half inches long. Once we had identified it we noticed they were around long after the other frogs had disappeared into hibernation ..

The green frog (*Rana clamitans*) , is of course, green with a lot of brown on its back. It has a light colored stomach. Males have a yellow throat and females a white throat. It is four inches long when fully grown. Its sound is like a low-pitched banjo.

The green frog is one of the "true frogs." These are frogs that have long legs and webbed feet as well as large eardrums. True frogs live in a semi-aquatic environment and often we find them in the middle of our grass areas, especially in those areas that hold moisture well, for instance, at the side of a hill where water retained in the hill slowly oozes at the base of the hill. True frogs lay a large number of eggs and to see a green frog egg mass makes one wonder how the female frog did it.

The northern leopard frog *(Rana pipiens)* is also prominent in the frog ponds as well as in the swamp. These are about the same size as the green frog but these have rounded spots on its back and sides. Variations of the leopard frog are found throughout the world and scientists trying to separate them into different species have a difficult time doing it. Probably the way the slightly different groups developed is through isolation where a single trait may become dominant over the centuries.

About ten years ago there were many discoveries of deformed frogs in the Great Lakes region. Living frogs were found with missing legs and multiple legs as well as deformed head structures.

Usually when a deformed individual is born it quickly dies but these frogs persisted into maturity. There was a connection made between the deformities and pesticides but this explanation seems to have been more speculation than actual. There was also a theory on global warming. One Canadian scientist believed that clear water should have a substance such as tea added to it to cut down on the solar radiation received by the frogs. Fortunately we have an abundance of frogs at Hawk's Nest and have never found one with a deformity.

A few years ago we thought it would be humorous to put a large plastic red flamingo beside the big rock in the upper frog pond. Once the flamingo was installed and its wings were rotated by the wind our dog Bear waded out to the flamingo and chewed it into pieces. We now have a much smaller plastic red flamingo and so far Bear dog has ignored it.

Toads also lay their eggs in the frog ponds and mature into four legged creatures. They are quite small when they leave the water and migrate to the ground below the deck and then migrate to other parts of the property from there.

Toads are dry and warty looking. They are slightly over four inches long when mature. We find many of them in the woodpile, which is stored below one end of the east deck.

Toads have horizontal pupils and prominent cranial crests so they are easily separated from frogs. When the tadpole toads are transformed into four legs they are only about an inch long.

Sometimes we find many of these small creatures along the footpaths down by the bridge.
Toad eggs are laid in strings where most frog eggs are found in clumps and masses. It is interesting to make a daily check on an egg mass and see the first signs of new life wiggling in its small enclosure. It is also interesting to see if the hatching tadpole is a toad or a frog.

I have also dug many watering holes in the brush areas around the deep woods. These are about four feet in diameter and twenty inches deep. The depth is limited by the clay hardpan below the surface. The hardpan also limits the depth of tree roots. These holes are filled with water throughout the year. They provide water for animals and a home for many frogs as well as a place for toads to lay their eggs.

THE CREEK

Lilley Run flows from south to north in the middle of our valley. It begins at a ridge created by a glacial terminal moraine, enters the valley, passes through our properties, cuts through another terminal moraine and flows into South Branch which flows into French Creek, which flows into the Allegheny River and eventually into the Gulf of Mexico. Just to the north is a divide. The streams on the other side flow into Lake Erie whose waters eventually end up in the North Atlantic Ocean.

As Lilley Run meanders through the valley it is joined by many lesser runs and rills. One larger run enters Hawk's Nest from the west ridge after crossing Al's open field. The other run is completely on Hawk's Nest property. It gathers water from the seeps below the Ridge Trail and is about a foot wide as it joins Lilley Run. Both of these streams never cease to flow, even during the driest times.

Lilley Run is six feet wide and on average eight inches deep. Where the new bridge crosses it, the stream is only two to three inches deep. There are many deep holes along its path as well as two beaver dams. The two beaver dams are at the south end close to Al's property. These are presently in good repair and the deepest water in it is about four feet. These dams are damaged from time to time and the beavers eventually get around to repairing them with mud, grass, roots, willow limbs, and rocks. I have often found live clams in the breastwork of the dams and I always put them back in the water. April and Matt have often went swimming in these waters.

A beaver dam near the bridge once backed up enough water to make part of the trail impassable, I tore the top part of it off to lower the water. The mass of intertwined twigs, limbs and mud was very difficult to untangle. Beaver skat, is fascinating. These are round and the size of golf balls. The composition of this skat resembles coarse sawdust.

Beaver (Castor canadensis)

At any given time there are at least a dozen beaver at Hawk's Nest. We can see them at night on their various excursions if we do not make excessive noise. Once they are aware of us they slap their tails and go under water.

Beaver are among the largest rodents in the world. Fully grown, they weigh from forty to sixty pounds. The largest beaver trapped by Jim in our valley weighed forty-eight pounds. A trapper may take eight beavers in a Pennsylvania season. Jim usually takes three but in years of plenty he will take five. Most of his beaver are taken from Al's property where a large dam has flooded what once was a good pasture. Nobody tries to destroy the dam since there are no longer any dairy cattle in our valley.

The beaver has large hindquarters and a small chest and forelegs. Its head is small but its jaws and teeth are powerful. It gnaws through trees peeling off a six-inch strip without difficulty.

A beaver's eyes and ears are small and its teeth are curved and long. It is a good character for cartoonists. The large enameled teeth grow continuously and the beaver needs to constantly use them to keep them from getting too large to be effective. Some trappers I have known maintain that if a beaver doesn't use its teeth they will become too large to cut trees and the beaver will starve.

The small front paws of the beaver have sharp claws which are used for digging. They also carry mud in their arms as well as their mouths. The hind feet are the size of a human with webbing between the toes. The second claw of the foot is a double claw and beavers are said to comb their fur and pick their teeth with this seemingly extra appendage.

The beaver tail is flat and covered with soft black scales. The tail I measured was nine inches long and five inches wide. The shape of the tail makes the beaver a champion swimmer.

The beaver is credited with opening up and populating western mountain states. Books, movies and legends tell thef history of trappers going west to get the pelts, which made many middlemen wealthy. The beaver trappers blazed the trails that most early famous explorers followed.

Beaver were one of the first animals to become extinct in Pennsylvania. The beavers were gone when elk, mountain lion, fisher, martin, and wolves still roamed the wilds of Pennsylvania.

Eventually beavers were purchased and brought back to the state in 1917 and released in Cameron County. The beavers came from Wisconsin, New York's Adirondacks, and the Algonquin Park of Canada. The rest is history. It took forty years for the beaver to find their way to Hawk's Nest.

When I lived in southwestern Pennsylvania the Game Commission released six beavers in Greene County. I was writing an outdoor column for the *Greensburg Tribune Review* at that time so I tried to keep a close check on the beaver. In the second season they were gone. I talked to a trapper who was setting out muskrat traps. He said he couldn't understand it but last year he had "trapped five beaver and now there aren't any." He blamed the Game Commission for their demise. He said, "Those people don't know what they're doing."

We have been at Hawk's Nest for thirty years and dams have been built and abandoned all along the stream. I covered one old curved dam with gravel and soil and use it as a road through one part of the swamp

There is one dam that has been here for the thirty years of our occupancy and it is repaired about every two years. The beaver never venture far from the stream. However, a group of them established a lodge in the pond five years ago and do not appear to be moving out.

There is an adequate supply of aspen and common poplar in the vicinity of the pond. Poplar species are the favorite food of the beaver. The trees replenish their numbers in a very short time. At this writing there are six large poplar cut down by beavers at the south line and eight at the north line. Several of these are hung up on other trees and will never fall unless I get out the chain saw and assist the beavers, which I frequently do. These trees are around a foot in diameter and were forty feet high before being cut. .

The beavers in the pond have a lodge four feet high and ten feet in diameter on the south shore. Its entrance is under water. Just off the entrance is a mass of limbs which the beavers have planted in the muddy pond bottom and on top of this they have piled more limbs. When Matt fishes in the pond he usually catches bass just off the edge of this buried treasure.

The stream beavers have a lodge on the bank. Part of the bank was hollowed out and they lived in this cave for a time. This bank lodge is approximately three feet high and eight feet in diameter. It is a work in progress. Beaver lodges always have an underwater exit.

Beavers appear to have a short memory. They will cut down a tree and abandon it. There are many isolated cut trees lying around the perimeter of the pond. There are also trees which the beavers have cut half way through and abandoned.

The beaver canal system is also a work of art. These are two feet wide and connect the pond, creek and swamp. Where there is a high rise in land the beaver will increase the height of dam to compensate for the difference in rise. Since the pond is eight feet higher than the stream the beaver have to make trails from one to the other. Eight feet difference in elevation is more than they can handle. The canals always lead from a clump of poplar to their dams. The lodges, dams, and canals are great engineering feats.

Beavers will take a section of mud and smear it with castor, which is a waxy smelly substance. Two glands, the size of Ping-Pong balls, on each side of the anus produce Castor. It seems to be some sort of communication to other beaver.

When we first admired the beavers they cut down one of my favorite wild apple trees. Since then I have put chicken wire around the trees I wish to protect. These include our one white birch, a tulip poplar, some apple and a few aspen.

There were some aspen I wished to preserve and since they were about a hundred feet from the pond I believed that they were safe. This turned out not to be true. They cut the trees and lugged the limbs back to the pond and made a nice beaver road doing it.

Trees favored by beavers at Hawk's Nest include polar, aspen, willow, apple and juneberry. They have cut ash and maple, but generally leave these alone after they have cut them. They ignore the hemlock altogether.

There was a large swimming hole in the creek created by a fallen tree. Water easily went under the tree, but when there was a heavy rainstorm or spring thaw the tree acted as a temporary dam. Somehow the tree precipitated hydraulic action fifteen feet upstream from it and a five-foot deep hole was created. This hole has served us well. Our children and their friends have enjoyed a refreshing dip here for many years. One of the rituals for children swimming in the creek is the check between toes for leeches. More often than not the leeches are there.

Leeches are not only parasites on humans but we have found them on snails, fish and turtles. They appear to be less than an inch long when at rest but once they stretch out they reach three to four inches.

When I wade in the pond to retrieve some debris I usually wear sneakers or footwear designed for a sandy bottom. On one such occasion I gathered some beaver cuttings that were in the way of our boat paths. When I got some branches to shore I noticed two leeches clinging to me. When I examined the limbs I found many leeches on them.

When we lived in the cabin while we were building the house we set out buckets of water at the swimming hole. We would skinny-dip in the hole, then come out and soap up, then wash off with a bucket of sun warmed water, then finish the bathing with a cool dip. We were cautious to move away from the creek when we lathered up so that no soap would enter the creek.

The stream teems with crayfish, many species of minnows, fly larvae and large fish. The bigger fish include native rainbow trout, stocked brown trout, chain pickerel and white suckers. Jim once caught a sixteen-inch pike in the stream on his side of the line.

Crayfish

No description of stream life would be complete without some mention of our crayfish *(Comborus barfoni)*. This crustacean grows to four inches when mature but there was a five and a half inch one in a shovel full of mud I was loading into my wheelbarrow. I put it back and procured my mud from another location. Most crayfish are light brown with a green tint but this big one was almost black.

Crayfish eat organic matter and small fish. I saw one with a fish in its pincher as it moved backwards in the creek. It kept moving until it was in deep water and I couldn't see it anymore.

Crayfish eggs develop on the female body and the young crayfish that develop cling to her for a while. Even after they release their grip they are tiny, but they look like the adult. They go through a series of molts until they reach their final size.

A crayfish may be observed by lifting almost any rock in the creek. Usually these are small crayfish and they scoot to another rock. The larger crayfish are probably picked off by raccoons.

One summer I caught two large crayfish, boiled their tails, added hot sauce and ate them. They were not spectacular, but it was interesting and the experience let me know it could be done.

We usually go to North Bend State Park in West Virginia on the third weekend in September every year for their Nature Weekend. It is a meeting of wild food enthusiasts. One year Ira Wood appeared with about fifty large crayfish tails, cooked up with his mystery sauce. His crayfish were better tasting than mine. I believe he added salt to the water.

Crayfish burrow deep on land and their holes fill with water. The holes probably go to those depths as a hedge against a dry season. One crayfish was dredged up from a depth of ten feet. Crayfish also create "mole hills." The crayfish hill has a hole in the middle of it where those created by moles do not. I have not observed many crayfish holes and chimneys at Hawk's Nest.

Two unique discoveries in the creek were the fresh water eels and a mudpuppy. The eels come back every year but we have only seen the mudpuppy once. Of course, we have a lot of other activities to do than sit on the stream bank waiting for a mudpuppy to appear.

The mudpuppy (*Necturus maculosus*) is a large salamander which when mature may be seventeen inches long. The one we saw was about that size. It stayed in the swimming hole for about a week.

The mudpuppy has four short stout limbs, each with four toes. Their main feature however, is three pairs of feathery red gills. It looks as if it has swallowed an old Easter Bonnet.

The mudpuppy eats fish eggs as well as fish. It also eats, insects, insect larvae, snails and smaller amphibians.

As to the eels, they come back every year and feed in clusters on rocky bottom of the creek. They work their way upstream. Five or six of them seem to all be digging at the same spot when we find them.

Our eels are the Northern Brook Lamprey *(Ichthyomyeon fossor)* and the American Brook Lamprey. *(Lampetra appendix)* They are non-parasitic and vary in length from five to eight inches. They have a long dorsal fin and a very soft body. They are easily caught by hand when they are clustered in the stream and mouthing rocks. The eels, like the black fly, are a sign of clean water. Eels are migratory and have a fascinating life history, which takes them out to the ocean. They die after spawning and their offspring return back to fresh water streams.

Black Fly

One of the horrors of spring is the emergence of the black fly *(family Simuliidae).* It is a resident of the creek where its thin white larva hide under rocks. The adult fly is about an eighth of an inch long. It injects a nerve deadening fluid as it bites so the victim is unaware that it is being bitten. A casual look at one's arm may reveal some oozing blood after the bite. A day later a very itchy welt will rise and last for at least three days.

The female of the species is the vicious biter. She uses the blood in her egg producing process. She will bite any mammal that comes within her jurisdiction.

Fortunately many birds eat the fly and fish eat the larva. However, the population is produced in such great numbers that there are thousands of flies around to pester us each season. To the east of us, the state sprays insecticide along the Allegheny River to reduce black fly numbers. We don't spray here but some of us wear insect repellent when we go outside during their peak season. Wearing a long sleeved garment also helps.

Raccoon *(Procyon lotor)*

One evening when we were living in the cabin and it was almost midnight we heard a ruckus on the cabin porch. There was a paper sack of dog food there and four small raccoons were tearing it apart. They were right under the window and the porch light was on so we had an excellent view of the action. We watched them for about twenty minutes. All of a sudden they became alert, looked around, then rushed from the porch.

Those little raccoons looked cute and cuddly but their claws are lethal. I discovered that one night when I was still in college and we went out to spotlight deer. We came across four immature raccoons on the paved road. I decided to catch one and I dashed out of the car and threw my jacket over one of them. As I attempted to roll the little guy up in the jacket he slashed through the back of the jacket and proceeded to tear other gashes in it. I no longer was interested in capturing him. It was another learning experience.

It was late August and we were still living in the cabin when we heard a voice call out to us. We went outside and Jerry was there with two of his dogs. He was wearing a battery operated headlight and was dressed in high boots and sturdy pants. He was coon hunting.

Jerry said he never killed the coons but enjoyed the chase, the baying of his hounds and putting the light on treed coons. On occasions the coon might leap from the tree and the dogs might kill it.

After Jerry and the dogs moved on we went to bed and listened to the dogs baying until the wee hours of the morning. It was a comforting sound. It was a memory of a bygone era lodged somewhere in our psyches.

My first experience with a coon at Hawk's Nest came on a walk in the woods with our first dog Lobo who usually trailed behind me snuffling in the side brush. I came upon a large raccoon on the slope below the Ridge Trail It moved slowly and deliberately away from me until it came to a medium sized ash tree, which it climbed. There was a three-inch slit about ten inches in length in the tree about ten feet above the ground. The coon moved until its head was parallel to the top of the slit and then it moved sideways into the slit and disappeared completely. A logger who visited our property told me that the tree was probably hollow inside and stated that this was peculiar to some ash trees that have been damaged by limbs breaking off. He also said that our giant white ash tree was probably hollow in most of its trunk.

Also on that walk Lobo and I came to an overhanging branch upon which was perched a Barred Owl. It looked at us and we looked at it. Generally Lobo was unaware of what was above her but she was aware of the owl. I watched it for about ten minutes, figuring it would fly away, but it didn't so I eventually moved on.

We have had many raccoon sightings over the years, most of them near water, and especially where brambles and brush divided the fields and woodlands. These edge areas are always teeming with wildlife.

A regurgitated owl pellet with a matchbook cover for size.

When Bear dog was two years old I heard him screaming somewhere near the big field. When I got to him he was confronting a raccoon less than half his size. The raccoon was trying to make it into a brush pile that was growing over with multiflora rose. The coon would turn to retreat and Bear would lunge at it and grab it with his teeth. The coon would spin around and snap at him. Bear would lunge forward with teeth showing and the coon would grab him by the lower jaw. They locked jaws. The coon would slash at Bear with its front claws and Bear would back off. There was blood on Bear's silver gray coat. I called Bear to come to me which he did. He is not as obedient a dog as I would like but he did come to me that time. He looked at me as if to say "Where in the world were you, I'm getting killed out there."

I removed my belt and slipped it under Bear's collar. As I led him toward his enclosure, I watched the coon bury itself in the brush pile. Fifty-pound Bear dog was no match for a twenty pound raccoon. Bear had a cut nose, a torn lip and a bleeding slash across his left leg.

One early spring day when Bear dog was older we were walking in the lower wet woods with snow still in many patches on the ground. I saw a raccoon about fifty feet away at the foot of a hemlock tree. I paused and tried to occupy Bear as the coon made its way up the tree. Too late. Bear spotted it and made a dash for it. The coon was about six feet from the ground. Bear made a great leap and knocked it down. They fought in the mud and I tried to separate them with my walking stick to no avail. Bear finally got it by the throat and held on until the coon was dead. With difficulty he carried it back to his lair. A few days later I tricked him into leaving it and then took it up to the gamelands where other creatures might dine on it.

Raccoons are found everywhere in the lower forty-eight states except in the Middle and Northern Rockies. These beautiful animals with their bandit mask and ringed-tail are one of the great favorites of wildlife enthusiasts. They prefer open woodlands, but will go anywhere the scent of food leads them. I had to give up planting sweet corn because they harvested it before it was ripe. A night trip to the garden with a flashlight in August always ended with raccoon eyes reflecting the light back at me.

A raccoon will eat just about anything that is smaller than itself. They eat frogs, crayfish, insects and especially grasshoppers. They will kill and eat muskrats and rabbits. They are as fond of acorns as they are of corn and autopsies indicate acorns to be their major food source where they are available. They also relish apples, grapes and beechnuts. When I visited a small winery twenty miles north of here the owner said he trapped raccoons and transported them miles away. He said that he was going to start shooting them and save himself a lot of time, gasoline, and aggravation.

City folks run into the raccoon when it raids their trash cans and pet food dishes. Some folks are thrilled to see the wild animal while others consider the coon a nuisance. On one of our frequent trips to Florida a coon chewed through a Styrofoam ice chest to get at a kohlbasi inside. On a later trip to the everglades we watched a raccoon by flashlight as it flipped the latch on a metal ice chest, lifted the lid, and started chewing into the milk and orange juice cartons stashed there. We were told that the Everglade campground coons had learned that trick and even taught it to their young. We then bought a small lock for the ice chest.

Raccoons are nocturnal and are rarely seen in broad daylight. If one is seen in the afternoon rabies should be suspected and the animal avoided.

Raccoons do not hibernate but keep denned up in the cold moths of January and February. This is also the mating season, which makes denning convenient. The young leave the den in June for short trips. They might accompany their mother when she pans streams for crayfish and insect larvae.

Raccoons are legally hunted and trapped in Pennsylvania and according to Game Commission data over a hundred thousand are "harvested" each year. Many raccoons tested positive for rabies one summer. Ever since that time we have become leery of raccoons. Of course, we keep Bear dog's rabies shots up to date.

There are some animals that always elicit awe and a thrill to see in the wild. The raccoon is one of these animals. It is always a pleasure to see a raccoon even if it is in our garden.

Opossum- pronounced possum *(Didelphus virginiana)*

Diary entry June 22 - Some excitement today. There was an opossum in Bear dog's enclosure. For some reason he did not know it was there until I let him out and he went around the outside perimeter of it. Perhaps it was outside and when he came around to get at it the opossum came through the fence which has four-inch openings. Bear was barking from one side of the fence and the opossum was on the other side lying on its back and hissing. It looked like it might be an albino at first glance, but it wasn't since it had those shiny, black, beady eyes peculiar to opossums. While hissing its long snout was open displaying rows of sharp looking teeth. There must have been fifty teeth in there.

Opossums are among the oldest mammal species on earth. Their ancestors lived during the Cretaceous Period (144-66 million years ago), which was at the time of dinosaurs and flying reptiles. The first mammals appeared on earth during the Jurassic Period (210-144 million years ago) but didn't start to increase and evolve in any great numbers until the Cretaceous Period.

Opossums are not fighters and their survival is probably due to their ability to eat almost anything, including probably dinosaur eggs. Perhaps they contributed to the demise of dinosaurs. However, due to necessity, their main food today is insects and carrion since these are most accessible to their lifestyle.

The opossum is a marsupial, which means that it raises its infants in a pouch or skin flap on its stomach. This flap covers the mother's nipples. The young are almost too small for us to see when they are born. They crawl in swimming fashion up to the pouch and enter to find a nipple to which they attach their mouths in a vise like grip. Those almost embryos that do not find a nipple die. A female may bear up to two dozen young but she only has thirteen nipples.

This opossum, mentioned on June 22 above, is the size of our smaller cat Abigail that weighs nine pounds. It has a prehensile tail, which is devoid of fur. Prehensile means adapted for seizing or grasping. The tail is strong enough to wrap around limbs and support the opossum as it moves through trees.

Opossums have been observed in all the environments of our land property. However, they can swim if they need to.

The opossum lives a hobo life adapting to most any shelter, perhaps a woodchuck hole, a squirrel nest, a tree hollow, or under a woodpile. It will eat almost anything. It lives a solitary life except during mating season. It does not hibernate but it does hole-up during cold snaps. There was one down by the big bridge in February a couple of years ago. It looked wet but probably wasn't in the creek water. I assumed hunger had driven it from some hiding place. I went back to the house and got some dry corn and put it on a cleared spot on the bridge. When I went back later to check on the situation there were many opossum tracks around the bridge and the corn was gone.

When an opossum is attacked or frightened it "plays possum" as everyone knows. Perhaps it faints. It is a survival ploy since playing dead might get it a couple of bites from an attacker but is then ignored.

My experience with opossums indicates they are not very intelligent. Its hearing is bad as well as its eyesight. Although, it does have a keen sense of smell. One year there was a dead woodchuck in the big field. As the woodchuck decayed it attracted crows and three young opossums.

Opossums are one of the common road kills on our Elgin Road. In some years one may see a half dozen flattened carcasses. Other common road kills on the road include woodchucks, gray squirrels, raccoons, rabbits, and skunks.

About three deer a year are hit by vehicles on the road. Last year there were four deer hit and killed. I didn't count the other critters but there were many of them. The front end of one car was so damaged by hitting a deer it had to be towed away. The owner later told me that the repair had cost over six thousand dollars.

Today there is a dead raccoon on the road. When I drove to the post office in Elgin there were two turkey vultures feeding on it. They became airborne on seeing my truck. When I returned there was only one turkey vulture. It flew into the air and as I passed I could see it landing back on the road through my rear view mirror. The raccoon had been moved from the edge of the road to the middle and I wonder how that happened. But I digress.

We are at the northern range of the opossum's territory although it does extend up to Lake Ontario and east to central New York State. It is of course plentiful in the south all the way to the Gulf Coast. Some possums were taken to the area around Los Angeles, California where they are now firmly established. Other than that, opossums exist in the wild from the Atlantic to Iowa. None are found west of Iowa or north of that state.

June 24 - (More on the opossum of June 22) The possum of June 22 is still with us. We put Bear dog in the barn last night since the possum was occupying his digs. When April went to check on the situation she found Bear on one side of the barrier and the possum sleeping on the other side in Bear's quarters. When I let Bear out this morning I saw that the possum had eaten his food.

Something had to be done with this possum, so I entered Bear's enclosure and put the reluctant possum into a small trash can and drove it up on the hill to the Gameland parking lot where I released it. It froze in place and I could see it had a gash on its left hind rump. Perhaps Bear did get a piece of it. Also the tip of its tail was missing. The injury did not hinder it from walking away from me. It should survive and have plenty of food since I had placed two road-kill raccoons there a few weeks ago and they were still there for the possum to eat. .

THE SWAMP

Lilley Run used to meander over the east side of the flood plain. Beavers aided in the meandering by building dams across the creek in several places, which caused the creek to change course and begin new meandering. When the dams were breached and the stream resumed a somewhat straight course this left the meadow with several isolated pools of water with a trickle of water running through them. By building a tractor road over one abandoned beaver dam and by blocking another trickle exit with the road I was able to extend a quarter acre swamp into an acre and a half swamp. Keeping the tractor road in good repair keeps the swamp in working order.

There are also small patches of marsh along the south line and a constant wet area in the brush below the house. A temporary stream enters the area and fans out. It was in this area [noticed a strange rock sticking out of the ground after the last snow melt in late March. When I went to pick it up the stone turned out to be the head of a snapping turtle.

Swamps, like ponds and lakes, are temporary features of the landscape. They will eventually be destroyed by filling in with sediment or decayed vegetation or by the erosion of their banks. Swamps are low spongy land generally saturated with moisture while ponds are open water.

Swamps and wetlands are vitally important to our environment. They prevent flooding by absorbing excess rainfall and slowly feed it into the stream drainage system. They regulate the flow of streams and have a greater variety of wildlife than any other land based environment.

Swamps and wetlands are valued as natural areas for this recreation and educational uses. They regulate ground water discharge, flood waters in storage, improve water quality, provide wildlife habitat, support the food chain and in many areas they stabilize the shoreline. During flooding an acre of swamp under one foot of water will hold more than 325,000 millions of gallons of water.

An experiment in the coal fields where I was raised had acid mine water running through a large field of cattails. I was told that when the water ran out of the field it was pure. I have no way of knowing the truth of that statement but I did see the field of cattails and the experiment. I was simply too young **to** grasp the meaning of it. My friend Ron Boone who worked for the Pennsylvania Department of Transportation said that he had read many papers on this method of purification. Many of them had positive results.

Another experiment near Philadelphia had sewage water running through another field of cattails. This too was said to purify the water.

However, we would not want to use any developed or historical swamp for pollution control. Pollutants, such as heavy metals and pesticides, would accumulate and begin to destroy the plant and animal life established there. Swamps should only handle minimum pollution occurring naturally in the area. Special wetlands, such as those mentioned above, might be developed to handle special pollution problems.

Unfortunately the valuable habitat of swamps, marshes, and fens is fast declining as developers drain those wetlands or fill them in. Fen is another name for a low flat lying marshy bog. It generally means a small bog.

Serious flooding occurs where there are no wetlands or where the wetlands have been destroyed. This flooding takes place throughout the world. These disastrous events can be traced to forest removal and the destruction of wetlands.

Our swamp is fed from water by the small stream that gathers at the base of the Ridge Trail, which is below a kame terrace. Water is also added to the swamp when Lilley Run overflows its banks. The overflow action must be closely monitored or else a gully will occur in the tractor road and the swamp will be severely drawn down. It takes a constant effort to keep the deep pools from being covered with vegetation. These pools are necessary for aquatic mammal and waterfowl movement. Newly hatched broods of wood ducks and their mother are often seen floating in the larger pools We have had a wood duck nesting here every year. Usually the hatch numbers nine or ten but one year I counted seventeen ducklings.

A local conservation club gave me two wood duck boxes about fifteen years ago. One was placed in the pond and one was placed in the swamp. The one in the pond never had an occupant. The one in the swamp was occupied for a couple of years. Both boxes disintegrated after six years.

I was also given a wood duck box for Hawk's Nest by a colleague of mine who made several duck boxes for demonstration purposes. The box he gave me was smaller than the usual duck box. I put it on an eight foot pole in a deep hole in the swamp. A cardinal immediately took over and built a nest in it. I was not around to see if the cardinal offspring fledged. I assumed that when they left the nest they would hit the water and drown. I never did find any dead cardinals as I checked the location on my daily walks. I assume they made it.

When spring arrived one year, and the mating season was on for birds, there was a cardinal perched high on a dead elm singing its head off about every ten minutes. It finally stopped, probably to adjust its vocal cords. I am not musically gifted by any means but I tried to duplicate the cardinal "what cheer" call. It must have been pretty good since the cardinal immediately responded. I answered again and a second cardinal answered from the other side of me and joined the chorus. It was interesting and the cacophony lasted until my energy in this matter gave out. I eventually left the scene and the cardinals to battle it out.

One early spring there was a blue-wing teal nest on a bank on the of the swamp. It was on the bank that separated the swamp from the creek. When the creek overflowed its banks the nest and its eggs were washed away

In and around the swamp live the cedar waxwing, cardinal, and rose-breasted grosbeak. The kingbird was a regular builder for many years but we have not seen one in the last few years. Muskrat nest mounds are found here. In winter the tracks of mink and gray fox abound. There is a large brush pile near the edge of the swamp and here is where the mink works out.

The brush pile is constantly being renewed with willow, red osier dogwood and viburnum cuttings as these species keep encroaching on the mower road around the swamp and must be cut back if the road is to be kept open ..

About two years after the swamp water level was stabilized I noticed that the stream coming down from the terrace was filling its entrance into the swamp with sediment which was in the form of fine clay and peat. If this continued, the swamp would be filled in within a very short time period. So I constructed a catch basin where the small stream exits the woods. This was a deep and wide excavation in the stream It collects the sediment and the clear water continues on to the swamp. This catch basin needs cleaned periodically. This has worked so well that I constructed a similar catch basin where the spring run enters the pond.

The fringe areas of the swamp are populated with Joe Pye weed, vervain, boneset, ironweed, goldenrod, bedstraw, swamp milkweed, yellow nut sedge, poison hemlock, water smartweed, reed canary grass, hardstem bulrush, carpetweed, and Spanish needles. Growing in the water of the swamp are elodea, American pondweed, curlyleaf pondweed, leafy pondweed, American frogbit, narrow leaf cattail, common cattail, watermilfoil, flatstem pondweed,and burweed.

Watermilfoil, coontail, and southern magnus have moved into the pond. Their growth in summer is phenomenal. They are cutback in winter by muskrats eating them and beaver using them for dam material. Much of the vegetation also simply deteriorates when the winter run cannot supply them with sustenance.

The appearance of the swamp pools differ than the appearance in the pond since the swamp vegetation, such as the pondweeds and burweeds are either floating on the water or projecting up through it.

There is a swamp in the woods where the land flattens out before the flood plain. It is a very wet place with pools of water surrounding small trees that grow to a height of twenty feet before they are blown over by the wind. Trees in this swamp include hemlock, blue beech, witch hazel, red maple, and poplar. There are also vines of clematis, Virginia Creeper, greenbrier, and poison ivy.

Matt and I enlarged two of the larger pools and I made a walkway through the center of it. We refer to this as the woods pond. We have seen raccoons on the dry areas. A Rufous-sided towhee nested here one summer. Several times, I came upon the scratching for insects in the dry leaves of the woods. I have not found a towhee nest in the last few years but its song of "drink your tea" resounds in the air every summer.

Painted Turtle

Once the swamp was stabilized, painted turtles (*Chersymys picta*) began to appear. They could be seen sunning on logs floating in the deep pools of the swamp. I counted six on one log a few years ago. On that same day there were four others scattered along the edge of another bank near a deep pool.

The upper swamp water level is maintained by two four-inch pipes under the tractor road. The lower swamp level is kept constant by a six-inch drainpipe, which leads to the creek. On the upper outlet there are two pipes, one is located three feet deep under the tractor road and the other is a straight pipe six inches below the road surface. I installed the deep pipe with a shut off valve in case I ever wanted to drain the swamp pools.

One day after a heavy rain I found a dead painted turtle upside down in the downward drain. After that episode I drilled holes in the sides of the pipe and strung wires across it. After another hard rain I found a turtle caught in the wires, but it was alive. Eventually beavers covered both pipe entrances with mud and water plants. I cleared the straight pipe and left the downward pipe covered. I can always open it if the need should arise.

A painted turtle is seven inches from head to tail. It might grow to eight inches if its genetics permit. They have a smooth shell with red and yellow markings. These marks are on the legs and neck. They are timid creatures that will live in an aquarium if it has a landing platform. We have picked up several migrating painted turtles along the roads of the area and have brought them home to Hawk's Nest.

Painted turtles eat insects, snails, mosquito larva, carrion and crayfish. The female lays eggs on land near the water. Some females lay eggs in two sets of holes at different locations. It must be a practice that leads to maximum survival.

Swamp Salamanders

One of the surprises of the wild is that one can walk right by animals without noticing them. Many times have I walked along a trial and only when I stopped abruptly did an animal emerge from its hiding place.

Finding the spotted salamander *(Ambystoma maculatum)* was exciting since we were at Hawk's Nest ten years before we discovered one. The spotted salamander is a large nine-inch amphibian with two rows of large, round, yellowish spots on its black slate body. These extend from behind the eyes to the tip of its tail. It is a reputed resident of the forest but we have only seen them in the swamp. Their swamp presence might be only in the breeding season.

Our other swamp salamander is the newt *(Novophthalmus viridescens)*, which can be seen swimming in every part of the swamp and in the frog ponds. It has red and black spots on its light tan skin. Its tail is strongly keeled. In its immature stage it is a terrestrial eft, a small orange salamander with red spots. It is found in large numbers in the woodland in summer. It is smaller in the eft stage than in the mature stage. After the eft stage it becomes a permanent resident of the water environment.

An orange colored eft climbs along my hand.

When I conducted field trips for summer school children they always enjoyed catching and releasing newts. They also were thrilled to catch and handle the little brown snake. These experiences provide a rational concept of the relationship of creatures in the environment and allays some fear of nature.

Canada Goose

In the early years at Hawk's Nest the Canada Goose *(Branta candensis)* made nests on two small islands that I had constructed in the swamp for that purpose. The islands were made by digging mud and piling it. This had the double benefit of creating the islands and making the water around it deeper. The islands are eight feet in diameter and two feet above the water surface ..

Many of the avian Canadians now stay in the area throughout the winter but they are not seen at Hawk's Nest. They hang around the grain fields near Lake Erie. Most of them, however, migrate to their winter feeding grounds on the coasts of the Carolinas.

Each year one pair of geese returns before the ice has melted on the pond. They return before daylight and announce their presence with loud honking, which prompts Bonnie to announce that "the geese are back." When daylight appears we can see them walking on the ice and dunking in the water at the exit hole of the pond's main drain. They go to the swamp in the evening.

After the ice melts several other pairs of geese arrive on the pond. They also use the beaver ponds in the creeks. The geese feed in the swamp. Most of them go upstream to the flats at Farmer Al's to nest. Two pair usually nest somewhere in our swamp. The earliest geese to arrive begin nesting immediately and are often nesting with snow all around them. Many times we have seen a mother goose on the nest with snow falling in large wet flakes on top of her.

When the ice has left the pond the territorial geese wars begin. As many as thirty geese might be on the pond at one time. After a couple of weeks they may be down to six pairs. Those that survive the. cut usually go upstream to the beaver dam areas. They are constantly in the air every day with honking and flying low over the brush. When we walk around the pond the more skittish geese take flight and head for the swamp.

Geese leave a lot of nuisance droppings behind. The droppings begin to diminish once the nesting season is underway. At two local golf courses the keepers go around smashing goose eggs during the nesting season.

We find hundreds of feathers around the pond and swamp when the adult geese begin to move upstream. We also find many mature geese and their goslings resting on the mower roads around the swamp during molting. However, most of the geese move upstream until their new feathers come in. Even after the goslings mature they still swim in a line with one parent at the head and one guarding the rear.

In spring and autumn the migrating geese can be seen flying overhead in their familiar V formation. Many of these flocks contain over a hundred individuals. They fly north in the spring and south in autumn. If they didn't honk they might pass overhead without notice. Such is the case with whistling swan migrations. Many times I have looked up at the sky and seen large formations of swans. Sometimes the swans start calling their cronk cronk signal, which sounds like a squeaky rusty gate. Otherwise they would also pass overhead unnoticed. Geese are high flyers. One was seen from a commercial aircraft, which was flying at twenty-nine thousand feet.

The Canada Goose with its long neck, gray back, white breast, white neck and black chin strap is unmistakable. There are reputed to be several races of these birds but this splitting of hairs is best left to the experts who do such things.

Mink

Everett came up from fishing in the creek one evening and said he had seen an otter in the swamp. He wasn't able to get a good look at it but he thought it was an otter. The Game Commission did release otter some fifty miles from Hawk's Nest and it was possible they could have migrated here. However, it seemed unlikely.

A few evenings later we both went to the swamp and saw a mink. Everett decided that he had seen a mink and not an otter. The mink are secretive creatures and we don't see them often but we do see evidences of them.

The mink *(Mustela vison)* is approximately fifteen inches long and its tail adds another nine inches. It is dark brown. There is no seasonal color change.

There was a mink den on the slope below the Ridge Trail. It was in and under the roots of a hornbeam tree. The den was identified by mink droppings. I found a half-eaten white sucker fish near the entrance. Although I spent considerable time watching the den I never did see the mink enter or leave.

Jim sets his traps in the pond, the swamp and the creek. He only catches mink in the swamp, especially around brush piles near the water. Jim usually harvests around five mink during trapping season. They are one of the most sought after animals. The average mink weighs about five pounds. It takes a lot of its luxurious fur to make a coat. The mink fur is usually used as trim on other fur garments.

The mink is a nocturnal creature that travels alone. If it is cornered it will emit a strong odor. It will also hiss and scream. It has a distinct bark and can be recognized in the territory by this sound. It also emits a purring sound.

Mink is a predator and its favorite prey is muskrat. It eats crayfish, snakes, clams, fish, and carrion. They will capture rabbits with ease. It is said that a mink in a chicken coop will kill all the fowl before it leaves. The mink is known to store carcasses in different places.

Mink will pursue a muskrat under water. There have been reports that a female muskrat with young to protect will usually fight off a mink.

My best experience with a mink occurred one evening when I was sitting down by the bridge near the old swimming hole waiting for bats to emerge from under the structure. A mink climbed down the bank from the direction of the swamp and swam across the swimming hole, climbed out of the water then walked up into the brush near me.

Star-nosed Mole.
Lilly Run often overflows its banks when the spring thaw is accompanied by rain. It was such an occasion when I crossed the old bridge to see if the trail around the swamp was being washed out.

When I arrived at the low spot on the trail it was under two inches of running water. I had my boots on so there was no problem with crossing it. When I got to the other side of the running water area there was a small animal running ahead of me. It was a star-nosed mole and it half swam and half ran through the next area, which was also under about two inches of water. The mole was probably flooded out of its tunnel. A week later I found a dead star-nosed mole in that same area. I had my video camera with me and captured about five minutes of it on film ..

The star-nosed mole (*Condylura cristata*) is the only American mole with a long tail and the only animal in the world with a star nose. The star nose is created by a group of short, pink, tentacles surrounding the snout. There are eleven tentacles on each side of the snout. Except for the tentacles the mole is dark brown. It is five inches long and its tail adds another three inches to its length. The one I found had a swollen tail, which is some kind of fat storage organ, like a hump on a camel.

The front feet of the star-nosed mole are quite large with five large claws that are used for easy digging in wet earth. Its food consists of beetles, various larva and whatever edibles it can find including slugs, snails, and perhaps carrion. I found one star-nosed mole under a dead deer carcass. It was probably after the maggots and not the dead deer.

There are whiskers on parts of the mole that act as sensors when the mole moves through its tunnels or to a new area. These sensory organs help the mole determine whether it should proceed in a certain direction or retreat. The mole eyes and ears are quite small. However, the animal's inner ear is quite large and sensitive to sound.

Since the star-nosed mole demands a swampy terrain, it likely would not be a lawn pest. This is assuming that people do not have large wet spots in the lawn.

The mole not only digs for its food but also may swim for food in ponds and swamps. They have been caught in muskrat traps.

A star-nosed mole is likely to turn up wherever there is an abundance of earthworms such as in wet sawdust, fresh manure, or under grass clippings. The star-nose mole migrates at night for obvious reasons.

The star-nosed usually tunnels along while pushing earth above it making the soil bulge. Once I learned to recognize their tunnels I began to trace their movements. These seem to be random, They always keep to wet soil areas. They will on occasion make a molehill when they dig vertically instead of horizontally. Their molehills are not as profuse as those of other moles.

INSECTS

Insect species are too numerous for anyone individual to know them completely. It is a brave entomologist who attempts to write a book on insects since they are very diverse with a complication of families and genera. Most books written for the general public can only touch on the various categories of insects. Books for children can only list a few of the common species and most likely those found in the backyard. Beetles alone, according to Borrer and White,in their Peterson Field Guide have 290,000 species identified and cataloged. The species of beetles in the United States number 28,600. It takes a large number of cooperating entomologists even to begin to understand their relationships.

As a college student interested in biology I began a bug collection with pins, nets, the works. It became too time consuming and when I looked at the feet of many of the insects under a microscope it was too visually disturbing, especially the house fly.

Insects dominate the earth. Three fourths of all the animal life on earth belong to insects. So when I comment on insect life at Hawk's Nest it is only a fraction of insect life that is here. I am constantly finding new species on the property, most of which I cannot identify and do not wish to spend the time doing so. I have mentioned contacts with insects in other sections but will add to the comments here.

In the preface to their book on insects, Borror and White state, "there may be more kinds of insects on an acre of land than there are species of birds in the entire United States, and their may be as high as several million individuals per acre."

When I began to write this section I thought that I would first write the common names of insects that came immediately to mind. When I paused from making the list I had fifty-seven names written down. Insects are every where. They crawl, fly. swim, burrow, bite, and sting. They are not all destructive; they help in soil production and plant pollination, which is very important. Many insects keep the harmful insects under control.

We do not spray for insects at Hawk's Nest. We know that if you destroy mosquitoes and flies you also destroy the food base for birds, fish, frogs and toads as well as many other creatures. We encourage birds and bats by building sanctuaries for them. In the twenty-five years of living in this house I have never been bitten by a mosquito while sitting out on one of the elevated decks.

When we first obtained the boat Everett and I went fishing on the pond. Everett remarked about the large reddish mosquitoes that passed over us occasionally. It finally dawned on us that they were female mosquitoes filled with our blood. Only the female mosquito bites.

We attribute the lack of mosquitoes around the house to our encouragement of insect eating birds as well as bats. Two different pairs of phoebes come back to build a nest on and under the deck each year. Barn swallows always have at least one nest on the porch rafters of the lower deck. Our bird boxes have bluebirds, tree swallows, and wrens in them. Our nearby trees have had nests of yellow throat and yellow warblers. These keep the flies and mosquitoes in check. The big pest this past summer has been carpenter bees, which look more hazardous to humans than they really are.

For several years we had the large basketball sized paper wasp nests under the deck and on the house eaves. The bald hornet builds these. The nests on the eaves cause no problems but those under the deck cause apprehension as their builders move about on and beneath the deck. We consider the nests under the deck a serious matter. Yellow jackets also build nests under the decks.

Several times the ball nests reached ten inches in diameter before I decided to act on them. I would wait until sunset and the hornets had retired for the night and then I would slip a paper-shopping bag over them and run a plaster spreader over the nest to cut the anchor. Once the nest was in the bag I would curl its top sealed and take it to a far comer of the property, drop it, then poke a hole in it with a stick and beat it out of there.

The true paper wasps build the paper combs that are attached to high dry places on a building. The paper is made of chewed-up wood. It takes a lot of mouthfuls of chewed wood for wasps to build a comb. We get a lot of them every summer. We usually leave them alone unless I have painting or repair chores to do in their vicinity. These nests usually clog the screens in the corners of the barn roof.

Except for the queen, the paper wasps die off at the end of summer, at least that is the expected way of nature. It was in February when I put on my boots to go out in the snow. There was a paper wasp in my left boot and it stung me. It caused me to invent a new form of dance.

The really bad stings come from the yellow jacket. When you live close to nature as we do it is inevitable that you'll be stung by yellow jackets. They seem to build in any accessible place, in crevices, underground, between loose boards and under porch railings. They hurt when they sting. I usually get a couple of yellow jacket stings every summer. One summer I received more than my usual allotment and had the left side of my face swollen for a week.

The carpenter bees are having a good time this year. They drilled holes in the facia all around the house. They do not sting but their large size scares the unfamiliar. Hitting them in the air with a fly swatter only knocks them down. They get up and fly again. Hitting them with a thin piece of wood keeps them down.

A hairy woodpecker visits the house from time to time and it probes the holes made by the carpenter bee. Sometimes it enlarges the holes. Other times when it works near the rain gutter, the metal acts as a sounding board and their pecks are amplified.

The hairy woodpecker has also sought other insects on the house and have pecked away a small area of the siding on the south facing side of the house. This will need replaced.

We have a potted flower garden consisting of various sized containers on the east deck. These are visited by bumble bees and humming birds. We do not disturb the bees or the birds when they visit and they do not disturb us.

The bumblebee is a fascinating creature. It lives in colonies with a queen, male drones, and workers. When a scouting bee finds a new source of pollen it will go back to the hive and with a series of dances will tell other bees exactly where the new pollen source is located. Honey bees also perform this informative type of dance.

The bumblebee is a large bodied black and yellow insect. It has pollen sacs on its legs. It has large elongated mouth parts which makes it the only insect capable of pollinating red clover.

Our mowed lawn and the mowed roadway around the pond are loaded with white clover. For the first fifteen years of living at Hawk's Nest it seemed like every clover blossom had a honeybee on it.

About eight years ago a fungus invaded the hives and killed off most of the honeybees. Only the bumblebee was seen on the clover for the next several years. Now the honeybee is making a slow comeback. I counted sixteen of them in a quarter-mile walk on the pond road on one day last week. That may not seem like much but it is a lot better than zero. The pollination of flowering plants is worth a whole lot more than the honey that the bees produce.

Honeybees are wild and domestic. They have been raised by humans for centuries. Honey combs and furs were the principal trade item in early history of the Volga River and the Black Sea.

We can judge the health of honeybees by the number that appear on our white clover which is abundant on our mowed areas. When the queen bee moves, the colony of drones and workers go with her. She always leaves a new queen behind to start another colony.

It was in the first week of November when I noticed two blue aster bushes loaded with honeybees and bumblebees. What was interesting about this was that we had four hard frosts and a six-inch snowfall the previous week. So the bees did not perish in that cold period.

I followed the advance of the gypsy moth for many years. It began with an escape from confinement in New England in 1869 and made a progression westward at the rate of twenty to forty miles a decade. It will eat leaves and needles of more than five hundred different plant species.

About twelve years ago I noticed thin small light brown egg masses attached to the bark of some aspen trees. Along with the egg masses these were many inch-long moths with a light buff color and irregular dark markings on their wings. Two years later we had a gypsy moth infestation.

The larvae were everywhere. We couldn't use our picnic area, which was nestled among poplar and wild apple trees. Little Matt would not use the tree house that I built for him. He went around mumbling how he hated those 'gippy mots.' We simply had to wait them out.

We waited for the onslaught of gypsy moths the following year. It never came. A virus had infected their population and virtually wiped them out in our area.

From time to time we get a high population of a particular insect. This lasts for a few years then there is a decline. We had an abundance of praying mantis for two years . Their large egg cases were all over the lower part of the barn as well as on plant stems. They seemed to be everywhere. Then they too went into decline.

Another insect, which was rather obscure until it exploded in the area was the bee fly *(family Bombyliidae)*. We came home late one evening and about three dozen of them were on the porch under the lamp. It was an unfamiliar species and I suspected some stinging, biting creature. However, the next morning they were gone. A few showed up a few days later.

Friends had come to visit and we went biking on the Allegheny River Trail, which is an old railroad bed that parallels the Allegheny River. There were several dozen of these same bee flies where the Allegheny Trail crosses the Sandy Creek Trail. They looked dangerous, but we watched them for about twenty minutes before we pushed on. They flew low around the cinders on the side of the railroad bed. We saw the entrance hole to their nest in the middle of where they were swarming ..

These bee flies were about the size of the mud dauber wasp but much thicker bodied. Their wings were transparent with many black patterned markings. When they landed their wings were outstretched. They looked like trouble but I have since learned that they do not bite and their larvae are parasites on other insects. After that one year I don't recall ever seeing another one.

When the Asiatic ladybugs first appeared in our house about eight years ago we were very careful to nurture them and give them the same courtesy that we gave the common American variety. They were more elongated than our variety. The Asiatics are orange and yellow whereas our common variety was red with black dots. We welcomed them anyway. A few years later they had worn out their welcome.

Articles on how to remove ladybugs appeared in newspapers and they were discussed on TV news programs. We began to remove the screens on our windows and force them out. We sucked up those that wouldn't leave or were in other parts of the house with the vacuum cleaner nozzle. There were thousands of them in the cabin, which was unoccupied. The Asiatic ladybugs seem to be under control at this time although hundreds appear inside our windows each spring. They really have worn out their welcome.

Another insect that needs mentioning is the mound ant. Their mounds are masses of fine grit and soil intertwined with grass roots. The mounds are built to a height of two feet with a diameter of up to twenty inches. Most of them are built along the tractor trails, along the pond, and in open areas of the field. When they start a new colony in the mowed area there is a cloud of dust as the mower chops off the top of the mound. The ants will persist in building but after three cuttings they give up and presumably move to another location.

The complete mounds of the ants contain many tunnels, white bread masses, and hundreds of ants. The ant that makes the mound is dark brown and four millimeters in length.

We also have a translucent pale tan ant that is two millimeters long and a brown variety about the same size. The four to six millimeter ants include a red and black, a black, a dark brown, and a light brown. There is a somewhat larger variety of black ant and once in a while I discover carpenter ants between boards down by the swamp. They are also in old wet logs. The carpenter ants need a lot of moisture.

I have put old lumber across a small depression near the swamp and covered it with old shingles and tarred paper removed from the cabin. I expect wildlife to move in. Preliminary inspection already identified many insects as well as the brown snake and a mouse. I will continue to monitor and record the wildlife moving in there.

Closely related to the ants are the termites. I brought some winged termites home in some gravel I scraped up along a country road. I wanted the gravel to fill in a depression on the pond road. Winged termites and winged ants appear in summer. They make their flight, mate, lose their wings and settle down to enjoy their life

Some people have trouble separating the ant from the termite. The termite has a body that appears in one piece while the ant is obviously segmented. Ants have a definite triangular growth sticking **up** their thorax and abdomen.

It was in August when we noticed a bleeding hole in Lobo's left shoulder. The blood oozed onto her white fur. Our first assumption was that it was a puncture wound. Then we looked at it closer and thought it might have been made by a pellet gun. Anyway a trip to the veterinarian was in order.

The vet took one look, reached for a thin pair of tweezers, and extracted a half-inch fat larva from the hole. He said it was a bot fly larva.

My idea of bot flies was that they enter the nostrils or mouth of large hoofed mammals and lay their eggs, which hatch into larvae that migrate to other parts of the animal. The warble flies also do this. It seems that the flies do lay eggs on the host and they penetrate the skin to feed.

The bot fly and blow fly are two insects that are drawn to deceased mammals. They provide clues to forensic pathologists as to how long a body has been in the outdoors. The larva goes through stages of development that an entomologist can identify almost to the hour. Thus, the pathologists can pinpoint the time of death in the outdoors with unbelievable accuracy.

Lobo and Bear dog have both had wood ticks on them. Ticks are not insects and are related to spiders. However, when people think of insects they throw the spider and ticks into that category if there is no fussy biologist to correct them.

Once April said there was a piece of gray plastic imbedded in the skin of Bear dog. When I checked, it was a tick swollen with blood. I removed it with my heavy-duty tweezers.

Every house contains hundreds of insects and arachnids. Every once in a while some spectacular insect such as a katydid, field cricket, leaf hopper or weevil gets in where we can catch it. We keep a viewing jar handy for the purpose of observing and identifying strange species

Bruce often quotes some European scientist who once said, "people are never more than one meter away from a spider." I have found this to be true.

Some quick insect stories.

There were black elator beetles in my clothing on the floor of my closet. These beetles appeared every spring for about ten years. Once they appeared I would check the clothing, which were clothes that I wore outdoors and didn't want them on hangers. These were laundered and would not have an odor about them. So what attracted the beetles?

I would pick up the beetles with a tissue and crush them with my fingers and deposit them in a wastebasket. There were probably a dozen each year. Sometimes they would leave the closet and fly about the bedroom. They haven't returned for the last two years and I assume I got the breeding stopped.

On our way to feed bread to the turtles and fish I often stop and catch a wingless grasshopper or cricket and throw it with force into the pond water. In a few seconds it becomes a snack for a Largemouth Bass or Blue Gill.

One of the pleasant memories of the swamp was seeing a light green luna moth flying erratically across the swamp at a height of about eight feet. It looked like a green bird. The moth has a wing span of five inches. Its wings have an elongation on the lower end resembling a tail.

A few days later there was a cercropia moth flapping on top of the swamp water as it came to halt on a floating pondweed leaf. It was too far out for me to rescue without removing shoes, socks, and trousers. About a half hour later I put on waders and went back to it but it was gone.

The cercropia is our largest moth with a six-inch wingspan. When I was a lad I brought home a cocoon and put it in my dresser drawer. At the time I didn't know what it was. Imagine my surprise when I opened the drawer one-day and found a large moth flopping around. I didn't know how to handle the situation but informed my mother about it as I set it on one of her begonia flowerpots. I don't remember the outcome of that adventure.

THE CABIN

Ever since I was old enough to be on my own I have had some sort of structure in the wild. As a teen I often went into the woodlands near my home and built lean-to structures where I would pass solitary hours contemplating the meaning of life.

When I first bought the Hawk's Nest property I would camp on it. Sometimes my friend Bruce would accompany me and we would camp and build a cooking fire. Curious neighbor kids would stop by and exchange stories with us. This was a good opportunity to size up the neighbors based on the demeanor of their offspring.

Eventually I ordered electricity and built a one-room cabin with a sleeping loft. The bottom floor was twelve by sixteen feet. The height of the slanted roof over the sleeping loft was an even six feet.

Irene and Everett would come north and use the cabin. Everett would fish in the creek. They would drive around the countryside and often visit the Allegheny National Forest, which is forty miles away. Bonnie and I would stay at the cabin. We would make forages into the city of Erie to visit the Playhouse, go to a movie, or swim in Lake Erie. Bonnie joined the local YMCA in order to use their pool and shower. .

It was the second summer when we made a late visit to the cabin and noticed two bird nests on the outside of the sleeping loft windows. When we went to sleep on the mattress which was on the floor a bat swooped over us. We opened the window and the bat eventually found it and exited. We lay back to sleep.

We both slept lightly and Bonnie said she felt like she was being bitten. We turned on the light and with the additional aid of a flashlight noticed the bed was full of little red mites. It was too late to do anything about it so we went to the first floor. She slept on the sofa and I slept in the easy chair with a footrest. The next day we took the bedding to the laundry and ourselves to the showers at the YMCA.

In the third summer of the cabin we brought six oriental college students to Hawk's Nest, three males and three females. Jerry loaned us a large tent. That and our small tent housed Bruce and the six students. Bonnie and I slept in the loft. Jerry also brought over two horses and saddles for the students to ride.

Everyone had a great time and the students are still in touch with us today. Two families came to visit us from Japan and a Chinese family visited us from Taiwan. We went swimming in Lake Erie, picking peaches at a farm on the lake, roasting potatoes and corn over a campfire. The weather was very cooperative.

Everett and I added a lower bedroom for him and Irene. Then we added a small sleeping room and a kitchen. We still used the two outhouses I had originally constructed.

A bat moved into an area between two roof joists on the porch. We named it Arnold. A woodchuck dug a hole outside the cabin. We named it Elmo, and so it went. We were in tune with nature. Our dog Lobo enjoyed it as much as we did.

Eventually we decided to move permanently to Hawk's Nest. I would take an early retirement from college teaching and perhaps get a job in the area to supplement the retirement . We purchased an additional two acres from Al and Grace and we lived in the cabin while we built the house. Our daughter April was one year old.

After moving into the house the cabin was not used. On a couple of occasions my nephews visited and stayed in the cabin. I hooked up a water system extending from the house. The nephews didn't make a habit of visiting and the cabin became another landmark without use.

Seventeen year old Matt and a three pound bass

was some expectation that daughter April and her friends would make use of the cabin. That did not happen. When son Matthew entered his teens he had friends visit but they didn't make a playhouse out of it either. They did destroy some its contents much to my dismay.

The cabin began to deteriorate and I made a valiant effort to keep it in shape in case we needed its use. The kitchen and small bedroom began to pull away from the main part of the building. I jacked the sagging floor joists and reinforced them.

The taxman came for reassessment of the property and declared the cabin as an extra dwelling. When I protested he said that the cabin was better housing than many area residents were using and we could easily rent it out if we wished to do so.

Since the cabin was not used and it was a tax burden, there was only one solution and that was to tear it down. Last summer I began removing shingles from the roof and board by board dismantled the living quarters. By the end of the summer I had the building down to the porch which I enclosed in order to temporarily house some of the furniture and other items I wished to save.

The dismantling did have some noteworthy experiences. I had the roof off and the flooring up and was resting on the easy chair taking a break and drinking ice water. As I sat there in silence a mouse started climbing the wall a few feet away from me. It had a little mouse attached to each leg. It rose to about three feet and then dropped back to the floor.

A couple of minutes later it climbed again with the little ones clinging to her legs. Instead of the previous route she went sideways to the window and climbed onto the sill. One of the little ones let go and the mother picked it up in her mouth and continued her climb until she reached a space on the plate between the rafters supporting the second floor.

I made a mental note where she had placed herself and as I tore down the second floor I left that part untouched until the mice were grown and able to fend for themselves. I was able to see them many times before they fled their nesting area on the cap rail between the rafters. They were larger than most mice and had beautiful light brown fur above and light colored fur below. They had big beady eyes and well developed ears. They were deer mice. (*Peromyscus moniculatus*)

Deer mice are rare to this area. Most state literature lists **their** northern range as Crawford County whose border is four miles to the south of us. I suppose a traveling mouse could make four miles if it wanted to visit a strange land. Exact identification was made when a pair of them came into the house last winter and were captured by our cats after much running from living room to relaxing room to kitchen. The house is well sealed and how they got in is still a mystery.

People who do not take the time to learn different species would probably identify our deer mouse as a field mouse. The deer mouse is brightly colored and larger than the common house species. The tail of the house mouse is naked and scaly where the deer mouse has a furry tail. The deer mouse eyes and ears are larger than the house mouse. It is a creature of the night.

Our deer mice are well fed since there is an abundance of wild cherry, poplar, hemlock, maple, wild grapes, snails, and insects for them. Deer mice will usually carry food to a dining location. It is common to find a place between rocks where the husks of maple seeds are cast about. It will store abundant seeds in its winter nest. It does not hibernate and when spring arrives their tunnels in the grass are apparent.

I have found deer mice in abandoned bird nests, which they had domed over and lived out the winter. I have seen these nests covered with snow. I have also found deer mice in the birdhouses when I cleaned them to get ready for the spring migration.

My first experiences with deer mice came when I had a previous cabin in the wild. Here I had a standing metal fireplace and on my lone weekend visits I would sit in front of the fire, drink a glass of wine and contemplate life.

I let the mice roam freely and on one occasion I woke in the morning to find a four-foot blacksnake curled up beside my mattress, which I always kept without frames and on the floor. I assume it was there after the mice and I hurried it down from the sleeping loft to the first floor. My cabin designs were always the same. They consisted of a first floor with an upper sleeping area under a peak. A porch always faced the best view.

One evening as I sat before the fireplace a very small mouse came up beside me. It looked like it was searching for its mother. The month was February and there was snow on the ground outside.

I put a piece of bread and a crumbled cracker on the floor beside me but the mouse went under the fireplace and apparently was trying to sleep. It stirred now and then. I went to bed and when I rose the following morning the little mouse was still under the fireplace. The fire had gone out during the night and the little guy was dead. He needed his mother's warmth.

Most of the furniture of the Hawk's Nest cabin was sold to a second land outlet on Route 6. The siding was sold to a couple who raised horses and wanted to add stalls in their barn. The plywood went to a high school teacher who was building a garage and the studs, joists, and railroad ties which supported he main building were purchased by a man who was building his own cabin. More than twenty rolls of insulation and much wiring were given away.

When I started tearing the siding from the peak there were about two dozen little brown bats dislodged. I would rip off a board and they would tumble out. Some were immature and others were not ready to fly. I gathered these and placed them in a cardboard box under the cabin. I monitored them each day and with some jostling of the box forced them to fly to the large maple tree near the cabin.

I constructed a large bat house and attached it to the electric pole, which was twenty feet from the cabin. I hoped the bats would find it. This would be a perfect refuge if it met their high standards.

The kitchen and small bedroom had come loose from the main building and the rain poured into the opening. It didn't matter since my wrecking bar and I were at it three hours in the morning and two hours in the evening.

When I got to the upper boards of the lower siding there were more bats. The siding was rough cut hemlock boards lapped one over the other and a good place for bats to hide and raise their young. Bonnie thought that perhaps we should keep the cabin as a bat refuge.

When I got to the lower three rows of siding there were no more bats, however there were many garter snakes. With every board removed a snake or two would fall out. These were all on the west side of the building. The bats were mostly on the north side. I never figured out the reason for this.

There were about twenty garter snakes of different sizes in the building. They all retreated under the porch, which I had retained for winter storage. When spring arrived this year I began to dismantle the enclosed porch after moving the stored materials to the barn.

One incident is worth mentioning. When I took apart the black fiber insulation from the headers of the window and door, there were thousands of dead Asiatic ladybugs and the area was wet. The stench was ghastly, like rotted fish. Immediately a couple dozen flies moved in and landed on the ladybugs.

I have stored the wood from the flooring and some other usable boards on slanted flats until I decide their disposal. I burned a couple tons of scrap wood, mattresses, insulation board and furniture. There is a lot of debris, which I refrain from burning, such as roof shingles and plastic pipe. Disposal of these and other material such as sinks will be a problem. I took ten large steel frame windows to the city of Erie for recycling.

The shingles that were over the enclosed porch were in a haphazard pile on the ground. When I went to organize them there were three large garter snakes and three small ones in the pile. I quickly placed three four-foot long studs under the lilacs that grew around the west end of the cabin. I covered these with siding and covered that with loose shingles. Then I directed the snakes to their new home. One of the large snakes went in the opposite direction but I felt certain it would find its way to the new snake house.

The cabin is no more. The happy times spent in that place are now a memory. I don't know how other family members feel, but I enjoyed sleeping there, probably more than I do in my comfortable ten-room house with one of the best state-of-the-art mattresses ever constructed.

There is always something interesting at Hawk's Nest. We walk almost every day on the two miles of trails with Bear dog faithfully at our sides. We notice the trees that are down by the wind and make a decision to cut them up or let them lay. We see new species of plants and animals and look for the old ones.

Visitors are welcome to explore the land. A representative from the Game Commission stopped by to ask if they could harvest our Mountain Ash berries since it was an American Mountain Ash. When I agreed to this he said he would deliver native trees of my choosing to plant at Hawk's Nest I ordered some red oak, white pine, and black locust. I will outline the property with these.

The Game Commission employees came and removed the ash berries to a height of ten feet on the twenty foot high trees. A few days after they left a flock of cedar waxwings came in and ate the remaining berries. I could not find one berry after they left, not even on the ground.

A representative of the Fish Commission stopped by to ask if I noticed some eels in the creek. When I said that I did he asked me to call him when I found them migrating up stream. He believed that a new eel species had entered his territory and wanted to confirm it.

It is my wish that my ashes be interred in the hallowed ground at the site of Lobo and Everett. It is truly a spiritual area of awe and wonder.

The Hawk's Nest forest and pond now belongs to daughter April and son Matthew. I hope they will continue to enjoy the property and when it is appropriate, eventually turn it over to their children.

The End

UPDATE

The photo on the opposite page was taken when Matt was about eight years old and jumping into the swimming hole which was about three feet deep at the time and the bank four feet above stream level. The bridge was constructed upon telephone poles supplied by Jerry Lindenberger. The surface was made of oak planks six feet long and a full two inches thick. These were obtained from an Amish two-man lumber mill in Spartansburg.

Five years ago there was a quick snow melt and the resulting flood washed the bridge downstream. As much of the bridge decking was recovered as could be had. The telephone poles were hung up and could not be retrieved without super effort. The bridge was rebuilt as a foot bridge in order to give easy access to the big tree area.

After the flood the beavers built a dam just a few feet up from the bridge. It backed up and inundated about three acres of land including the original large swamp. Deprived of plunging water the swimming hole filled up with golf ball and baseball sized glacial rocks due to erosion of the stream banks when the beaver dam occasionally overflowed.

An ancient Greek philosopher said it was impossible to step into the same stream twice. So it is impossible to step into the same area twice, except in memory.   JT May 2015

www.ingramcontent.com/pod-product-compliance
Lightning Source LLC
Chambersburg PA
CBHW070919290526
45795CB00001B/359